BALCONIES
AND
Roof Gardens

BALCONIES
AND
Roof
Gardens

YVONNE REES

WARD LOCK

For my daughter Natasha

A Ward Lock Book

First published in the UK 1991 as *The Art of Balcony Gardening*

First paperback edition published 1992

This edition first published in the UK 1996 by Ward Lock,
Wellington House, 125 Strand, London WC2R 0BB

A Cassell imprint

Text © Yvonne Rees 1991

Distributed in the United States by Sterling Publishing Co., Inc.
387 Park Avenue South, New York, NY 10016–8810

Distributed in Australia by Capricorn Link (Australia) Pty Ltd
2/13 Carrington Road, Castle Hill NSW 2154

A Library Cataloguing in Publication Data block for this book may be
obtained from the British Library

ISBN 0 7063 7460 6

Printed and bound in Singapore by Kyodo Printing Co

Cover photographs:
Jerry Harpur, designer Keith Corlett, New York City (front)
Jerry Harpur, designer Tim Du Val, New York City (back)

CONTENTS

CHAPTER ONE

GARDENING IN THE AIR

Not quite a backyard but more than just an architectural appendage, the balcony is a way of life; a garden room or superior kind of patio with the advantage of height and, frequently, a fine view. It might be outward looking, directing the attention irresistibly towards the spreading countryside or glittering city-scape beyond; or be more introspective, an enclosed and secret area, sometimes a fantasy miniature garden, enjoying a close relationship with the rooms within. A balcony may frame a window like an extended and decorative windowbox, or a door opening – screened by blinds, a blanket or curtain if the weather is hot or the location dusty – to provide a welcome access to what might be the only outdoor area the property can offer. Because it is suspended and separate, the balcony has something of a fairytale garden-in-the-clouds feel, like the land at the top of the beanstalk. It is remote, private, accessible only from the house, and to have use of one brings a sense of privilege and a great deal of potential pleasure.

A balcony can be beautiful: a celebration in wrought ironwork or carved timber and as much an asset to the building as to its owner. Then again, it might be quite basic in construction: a simple box or little more than a platform or ledge with a hand-rail for safety; or designed purely for decoration, little bigger than a windowbox or an ornate grille – perhaps simply an ornamental stone parapet over a bay window and only able to take the weight of a single plant container. Either way, for those with no garden of their own who perhaps live in a town or city apartment, a balcony becomes a private retreat, somewhere to grow a few favourite

Liberal use of white paint and a wonderful curtain of sweet-scented Wisteria *blooms makes it difficult to tell where the balcony begins and the porch or trellis ends.*

plants, an opportunity to sit out whenever the weather permits and a valuable extension of one's precious living space. Such privileges are much prized by the urban dweller.

Town or country dwellers lucky enough to have both a balcony and a garden – some houses and apartments can even boast a series of balconies opening off different rooms – may consider the feature in a slightly different light. They might treat it more decoratively and design the balcony as an extension to the appropriate living space – a kind of al fresco alcove, rather than their sole opportunity to create a small patio garden or backyard. Being rather spoiled, they may regard it with slightly less reverence and delight than those without gardens, but will still experience that feeling of owning something of real value. The balcony will still contribute a valuable and elegant outdoor extension to the available living space, especially when designed and furnished to harmonize with the room it adjoins. Sadly, too many people do not appreciate the balcony's full potential and abandon it to a few neglected pot plants and an open door during fine weather. This is especially true in towns and cities where the temptation is to shut out the noisy, grimy world outside, without realizing the advantages of good

Plain metal balconies provide a degree of decoration and a safety feature at the doorway or window of every simple white-washed house in this typical Greek island village.

screening and careful planting; nor the benefit of the balcony's limited size which means it need not cost a fortune to be stylish and create a glorious miniature environment in which to relax.

The balcony's external role should not be neglected either. For safety's sake it must be kept in good repair, and aesthetically speaking, if it is allowed to deteriorate it will spoil the whole façade. This is particularly important with the elegant Georgian and Victorian town houses of Europe's major towns and cities, but perhaps less so with Spain and Italy's flanks of balconies, where a slight air of sun-bleached dilapidation is part of their charm. Architecturally, balconies are essential to the appearance of their host buildings; a great many would look very bland or their windows blank and undressed without them. Where there is more than one balcony, perhaps in an apartment block, changing its style or appearance too drastically, or even using plants or tall trellis, can place it at odds with its neighbours. Once you are on a balcony, it is tempting to feel you are in your own private world with a new, elevated perspective on your surroundings. It is easy to forget that the balcony can also be seen from the ground, so it is equally important to consider how it looks from down there.

ANCIENT AND MODERN

Despite their add-on nature, balconies are such an integral part of buildings that it can be easy to overlook them from the street. That is a shame because it is fascinating to study the different types and styles of balcony even within a single street. Balconies have been used as practical yet ornamental architectural devices since the earliest buildings were constructed. It was the Greeks and Romans who discovered the technical expertise to build multi-storey buildings and developed the arch – a popular classical device for early balconies or elevated terraces. You will find balconies frequently used architecturally to dress up windows, to encourage a sense of symmetry or to provide a visual and decorative feature across the front of the house by linking two wings or bays.

The balcony as a stage

The effect of being raised above an audience, almost of being

Simple, small wrought iron balconies are often seen adorning the otherwise plain facades of white-washed Mediterranean buildings. With pots of brightly flowering pelargoniums crammed into every available corner, they are decorative as well as providing a valuable source of fresh air in a hot climate.

Opposite: Stylish choice of fixtures and furnishings can transform even the smallest roof garden into a delightfully comfortable extension of your interior living space.

on a stage, has meant some form of balcony has long been a popular feature of religious buildings. Examine the ruins of Greek temples like the Acropolis in Athens and you will often find a raised and roofed terrace or balcony flanked by classical columns or supportive statues – an ideal and impressive platform from which oracles could be proclaimed. Balconies were frequently incorporated into the design of churches and cathedrals too, such as the suitably Gothic style of Notre Dame in Paris, where narrow balconies at different levels offer breathtaking views of the city and closer acquaintance with the famous gargoyles.

Medieval

Castles and fortified manor houses have turreted battlements, which are surely an early form of continuous walk-around balcony offering a vital vantage point and also the only recourse to fresh air and exercise when under siege. You will also find Rapunzel-style ornate roofed and balconied windows that are decorative as well as practical in romantic medieval castles and French châteaux. Sometimes a carved or decorated balcony or series of balconies will create a stunning focal point on more ornamental early buildings, such as sixteenth-century Blois where the famous processional staircase spirals upwards behind a series of parallel balustraded landings to a matching balcony above.

In sixteenth-century England, timber-framed and elaborately pargeted buildings sprang up across the country, thanks to the rich purses of wealthy merchants, and were often expanded into whole rows of shops featuring an upper storey balcony overhanging the street from which to hang wares or throw slops. A surprising number survive today: book a room at The Feathers Hotel in Ludlow; one of England's most ancient towns, and you can enjoy the facilities of an extraordinarily carved and decorated wooden balcony, now beautifully restored and incongruously overhanging the parade of motor traffic through the main street.

The first floor balconied cloister, which echoed the private recreational facilities of castle battlements, became popular during the Renaissance. It was beautifully roofed and pillared and offered dry access between the upper rooms. Also combining fine style with a practical purpose in a city largely composed of waterways, the arched and balconied windows of many Venetian *palazzi* display a distinct eastern influence.

American

Balconies were often used as symbols of wealth, and so were a feature of the archetypal North American colonial house, perhaps based on Georgian-Palladian lines like Drayton Hall in South Carolina (built in 1738). Here an imposing portico with limestone columns is built on two storeys to create a fine upper balcony that is the central focus of the house. Balconies are a common sight among the elegant French-influenced houses of New Orleans too, and are beautifully shaded to provide a cool seating area and also protect the rooms within from dust and heat.

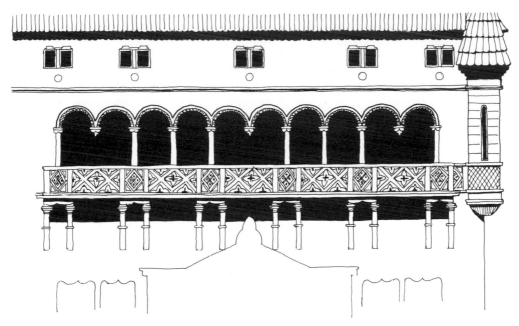

By the turn of the century; balconies were being built in a much simpler style, framed by plain metal railings and until recently relatively unadorned (now they are often ablaze with flowers and greenery). In fact, balconies never seem to have gone out of fashion but only changed their style through the centuries, and in some parts of the world where the climate and conditions make them almost obligatory, they don't seem to have altered much for hundreds of years. A balcony is as natural to a traditional seaboard home as it is to a country villa, or anywhere else with a particularly fine view or a hot climate.

An ornamental balcony running the full length of this Portuguese building makes an important architectural feature and gives cool, sheltered access between the upstairs rooms.

National styles

Balconies are an instantly recognizable trademark of the Mediterranean – hung with drying peppers or bright washing outside a Spanish town apartment, or a riot of geraniums on Italian villa or French farmhouse. Alternatively, they can be dark and secret, decorated with the carved shields and painted murals found on so many chalets in the snowy Alps. The typical European town displays a wonderfully rich variety of types and style of balcony: tiered on two, three, even four storeys, constructed in decorative wrought ironwork, carved stone or well-weathered timber. Sunny San Francisco is all the brighter for its multi-coloured display of striped and decorated awnings shading its many balconies; the more

Vigorous climbing vines and honeysuckle have helped to soften this fine example of ornamental ironwork, so that the architectural feature blends well with surrounding trees and shrubs and the balcony is afforded a little extra privacy.

A pretty cloth and a coat of paint are often enough to convert a simple table and a couple of chairs for outdoor use. Well-stocked plant containers and a leafy view may be the only other features required for enjoyable al fresco meals.

Brightly coloured awnings and ornamental balconies are a familiar sight along many wide, sunny streets of imposing seaboard homes.

restrained and sophisticated style of wrought iron is popular in Sydney; while Newport, Rhode Island favours timber structures.

Twentieth-century designs

The strong angular shapes of balconies have made them a natural choice for modern architects, and they are often incorporated into buildings as curves, wedges or other contrasting three-dimensional geometric shapes to add interest and variety. They were particularly popular in the 1920s and 1930s, when they were often designed as a sinuously curved profile incorporated in the main design, maybe as fat as a wedge of Gouda cheese. In today's apartment blocks all over the world they continue to be a stylish feature and a vital extension of the urban home. A separate balcony might be allotted to each window or designed as a continuous wrap-around structure on each level and requiring some form of screening or division for privacy.

The latest news is the landscaped balcony forming a series of staggered ledges and balconies which are specially designed to liven up the monotonous appearance of unrelieved glass and concrete. Once they have been carefully planted with a variety of evergreens, the building is somehow recontoured and softened to give the more natural impression, from a distance at least, of rock, hill and woodland. Such balconies can be wonderful living *trompe-l'oeil*, especially when blended with a natural landscape beyond. You can see them in the big resorts of the South of France, where they make the gleaming mass of hotel and apartment blocks more attractive, and they have now spread to the world's big inner cities, where buildings seem to have been draped in greenery like moss on a tree and add a little life and vitality to an otherwise sterile environment.

CHAPTER TWO

THE SKY'S THE LIMIT

STYLE AND FUNCTION

There is perhaps no other architectural feature capable of combining so satisfactorily both a decorative and practical function as a balcony. Decoratively, even the smallest, simplest balcony adds a touch of class or character to a plain façade, while a more ornate structure may be essential to the whole style and design of building, as we saw in the previous chapter. Size, shape, style and position will influence its use too, providing not only an enjoyable if limited al fresco addition to the home or office – the stylish patio or terrace with a view – but also a wonderful extension of the room within. With the doors or windows open, a well planned balcony can contribute a delightfully fresh garden atmosphere, a foliage-framed vista or an exotic jungle view, depending on one's taste and location. Whether out in the wilds or deep in an inner city, the area could be used to maximize the good fortune of a beautiful or dramatic setting or, in less desirable surroundings, create a fantasy escape from the real world.

ENJOYING THE AIR

On a practical level, the balcony may be an important, even

The jungle effect of packing lots of large architectural foliage plants together in pots and tubs makes a wonderful leafy view for any room in the house. Here plants have been used to shelter a hot tub, but they would have made an equally effective screen for an indoor adjoining bathroom.

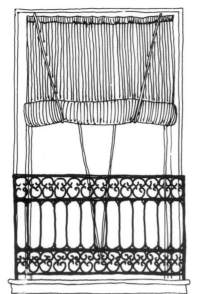

This small Spanish wrought iron balcony is primarily orn-amental but also supplies a welcome breath of fresh air through the open window, the cool interior shaded from dust and strong sunlight by a simple cloth blind.

vital element of home life, especially if there is no other access to a garden or patio and the climate is hot and sunny. Location and weather will to a large extent determine not just a balcony's style and type but also its day-to-day use. For example, the ornate wooden balconies of Austria and Switzerland are not purely for decoration. The weather may be mostly too crisp to linger outdoors for long, but on a sheltered side of the chalet, a balcony can be a suntrap and make a pleasant place to sit and enjoy brief, bracing bursts of sunshine, not to mention a breathtaking view. In more temperate climates, a balcony can provide greenery or a splash of colour, with pot-grown blooms and foliage, immediately outside an upper storey window.

In rural areas throughout the world, balconies will be found wherever there is a fine view and are equipped, at the very least, with some kind of seat but more likely with a table and chairs for al fresco meals and maybe a built-in barbecue too. In very hot countries, the balcony takes on an even greater importance as an overflow area from the home, especially in crowded cities. Here it might not only serve as a place to sit and catch a whisper of breeze or simply watch the world go by – and maybe provide the only comfortable place to sleep on airless nights – but also be the only area where washing can be hung out, or pets kept. The balcony is a popular place for city dwellers to install a small aviary, for example, with a built-in cage for ornamental or song birds which provide extra aural and visual pleasures. In downtown locations where conditions are cramped and facilities limited, the balcony may even be the place where the family cooking is done.

Practical use

The real beauty of the balcony lies in its adaptability. Visually and functionally it is equally at home in city squares or adorning rustic farmhouses; it might be a charming addition to a multi-roomed mansion or give some vital extra living space to each dwelling in an apartment block. It is a small private world which, when cleverly screened by plants, can take on any style and character you choose.

Size is relatively unimportant although, obviously, the larger the balcony, the more scope you have when deciding how to use and furnish it. Provided the structure is strong enough, however, it can usually be adapted to your taste and needs. Small has its advantages: fewer materials are required so you can afford to indulge yourself in more expensive ideas and furnishings to create a really stylish living area. Even the purely ornamental balcony – narrow and designed for maybe a couple of pots of plants but not human occupation – can become an asset and contribute to your precious moments of relaxation. If you choose plants and containers carefully, perhaps adding an ornament, statue or other decorative device if there is room, and designing it so the balcony opens directly on to one of the rooms inside, you can create a wonderful living backdrop and the impression of increased space. For the high-rise kitchen, a profusion of herbs will be useful as well as providing a sense of freshness if you have no garden, while a tiny flower-filled balcony could add much to the general ambiance and enjoyment of a small sitting room or dining room.

Setting the scene

The type and use of the room which opens on to your balcony area will also influence its design and decoration and, if you are being really elegant, the type and colours of plants and accessories you choose. This will not only encourage a continuity of style – and thus an impression of space – but will also affect the way the balcony itself is used.

THE BATHROOM

The bathroom balcony, for instance, will most likely be purely a leafy backdrop, a mass of greenery that acts as a wonderful living screen and makes frosted glass or curtains unnecessary, especially if plenty of large foliaged plants can create almost a jungle view. You could encourage this impression by using dramatic house plants inside the room too; perhaps a Swiss cheese plant (*Monstera deliciosa*), which has large, glossy broken leaves and is capable of growing right up to the ceiling, or a frondy Boston fern (*Nephrolepsis exaltata* 'Bostoniensis') – sometimes called the 'bathroom plant' because it thrives in a hot steamy atmosphere – which is perfect for hanging in baskets from the ceiling or standing on a classic pedestal or small table.

Carefully choosing the species and position of house plants

Sleek timber is smart without being cold and clinical: the perfect easy-care material for an inner city roof garden with a stark but dramatic view. Hardy evergreens clipped into geometric shapes and grown in pots help to overcome the inevitable problems caused by wind, dust and pollution.

will help to blur the boundaries between indoors and out, but only on the warmest days and evenings will the bathroom doors be opened so the owner can imagine he or she is bathing outdoors. That is why, in cooler climes, it is a good idea to provide the best insulated view of the balcony possible, with the help of double-glazed patio doors or picture windows and made-to-measure venetian or vertical blinds if screening or privacy is required.

THE KITCHEN

In contrast, the kitchen balcony usually has more of a practical than a purely decorative role. Frequently, in first floor kitchens, it forms a small platform or square balcony area leading to a fire escape or wooden or iron steps that descend to a shared garden at the rear of the building. For the convenience of the cook, or if the owner has no access to a garden, this can be a useful place to grow as many pots or tubs of herbs and edible plants as can be crammed together, so they will be handy for instant cropping beyond the kitchen door.

Making the most of the space

Arranging the containers at different levels maximizes whatever space is available; you can buy special multi-tiered containers or convert an old half-barrel to take a variety of herbs or a mass of strawberry plants. Alternatively, small pots of herbs can be wired to a trellis, provided they are supplied with fixed saucers for watering purposes or not allowed to dry out. If you have the room, tiered timber or metal shelves (greenhouse staging may be suitable, or even a series of brick-faced steps depending on the style and design of your balcony) will provide valuable extra growing space. Don't forget that hanging baskets, wall baskets and window boxes are all great space savers if fixed to the back wall or a stout trellis.

Herbs adjust well to being grown in containers and some, such as thyme, rosemary and bay (which makes a lovely ornamental bush or clipped tree), will provide fresh flavours all year round. More tender varieties may have to be brought indoors over the winter if the balcony is not well sheltered or the climate prone to hard winters.

A brilliant show of geraniums and petunias brings brightness to a traditional timber balcony in colder climes.

THE MINI KITCHEN GARDEN

It is also worth looking out for miniature and dwarf varieties of fruits and vegetables that can be container-grown and will provide the added attraction of flowers and fruits through the summer as well as fresh food for the dinner table. Tiny cherry tomatoes are ideal and can be grown in hanging baskets. You might also like to try growing miniature aubergines, dwarf courgettes or an ornamental sweet pepper plant that produces fruits in shades of red, green, yellow and purple which are as attractive as any exotic flower.

If the balcony is a real suntrap (and with its exposed position and the right screening this is quite likely), the high-rise gourmet can do very well indeed, with good yields and early ripening. Modern hybrids and varieties are specially bred to produce the maximum fruit from the minimum-sized plant; you may be able to pick up to 5 kg (10 lb) of soft fruit or tomatoes from just one plant. Depending on the size of your kitchen balcony, you could extend your scope from pot-grown herbs, tomatoes or strawberries to raised timber beds or boxes in which you can grow some quick-cropping salad plants – radishes, spring onions, Little Gem lettuces and perpetual corn salad are all ideal. Few experiences match the pleasure of pulling a handful of these vegetables for an instant fresh salad from your own backyard balcony.

Growing vegetables

If eating your own produce gives you a thrill, why not find space for a few vegetables too? Even potatoes can be grown in a barrel, or you could plant up grow-bags with a limited variety of compact vegetable varieties such as stump-rooted carrots or short-growing peas and broad beans. These bags are not particularly attractive, so if you want the area to look stylish you will have to disguise them in some way behind a timber- or brick-faced frame. You will also have to provide some form of drainage so the vital regular watering does not flood and ruin the balcony floor: specially designed troughs and trays are available for this very purpose. Runner beans, with their large green leaves and red, purple or white flowers, make lovely annual balcony climbers for a trellis or screen – the beans are almost a bonus.

Growing fruits

Fruits can also be grown in pots and trained against a balcony wall or trellis. The kiwi plant, *Actinidia chinensis*, is often grown purely as an ornamental climber but it will produce curious egg-shaped edible fruits given plenty of warmth and sunshine. Soft fruit bushes such as red or white currants, blackberries and loganberries, can be trained into flattened fan shapes along wires and blackcurrants could be pruned hard into a compact bush.

A sturdy balcony could even support one or two dwarf fruit trees; if the branches were trained along horizontal wires to produce espaliers and cordons they would take up very little space. Apples and pears are particularly suited to this treatment but you will need at least two compatible varieties, or one of the new multi-types grafted on to a single trunk, for successful fertilization. For hot sunny sheltered balconies, peach, nectarine and apricot trees can be bought ready trained into fan shapes, and the flowers and foliage are just as pretty as the fruits. In places where the winters are cold or the balcony is very exposed, fruit trees and bushes will need to be protected with sacking.

One popular patio and balcony plant is the citrus tree, which can be clipped and trained as a standard – a single

A rustic wooden balcony provides access to the garden via a simple flight of matching steps. A mass of plants in pots and containers makes a leafy link with the garden below as soon as you step through the door or look out from the window.

Minimum maintenance with maximum impact: the all-seasons appeal and tranquillity of an ambitious oriental-style theme featuring a dry stream made of pebbles and boulders and the occasional evergreen for architectural emphasis. Wooden staging on different levels doubles as seating and display for plants and ornaments.

straight stem with an attractive tight ball of foliage on top – and grown in a large terracotta pot or ornamental Versailles planter. These are so pretty that they are mostly grown for decoration and considered an accessory rather than a source of fruit, which is almost too attractive to pick. Because the pot or tub can be brought indoors during very cold weather, these trees can be grown on any sunny balcony.

THE BEDROOM

Busy with bees and butterflies and providing a wonderful blend of scents and sights with flowers, foliage and fruits, the

Interesting changes of level and a careful selection of trees and shrubs have made an otherwise dull area into a complete miniature garden environment at very little cost and trouble, and a perfect place to relax.

kitchen garden balcony is as pretty as it is practical. The *en suite* bedroom balcony, on the other hand, is redolent of luxury and indulgence – more usually enjoyed on holiday in a villa or hotel with a magnificent view of surrounding sea, mountains or countryside.

This is an area normally reserved for those spoil-yourself pleasures in life, yet those lucky enough to have a small balcony leading off a bedroom at home often do not use it to the full. True, a splendid setting is enough in itself to lure you out to view the stars in your pyjamas, but even if you are not that fortunate, good screening and the right furnishings on even the smallest, most unassuming, balcony will transform a quite ordinary bedroom into somewhere that makes you feel really pampered and privileged.

To be able to fling open the french windows or slide back the glass doors and reveal a secret, leafy enclosure scented with flowers, or even a fine sculpture framed by leafy evergreens, adds much to the enjoyment of a starry night. You may not even have to leave the comfort of your bed. If you add a small table and chairs, the balcony can be a delightful place in which to savour a leisurely breakfast on sunny mornings, giving you the finest possible start to the day. When the nights are hot and stuffy, some balcony owners even like to drag a mattress outside so they can sleep under the stars in the cooler air. On a small balcony shaded by a pergola or similar overhead structure, it is an easy matter to rig up some kind of mosquito-proof netting should it be necessary. Many people will even make this a permanent arrangement during the summer months, installing a comfortable couch or lounger that can double as seating during the day.

THE OUTDOOR LIVING AREA

If a building boasts serried ranks of balconies, the owner might be spoilt for choice over which one to use and when. The most common and profitable place to site a single balcony, however, is adjoining the sitting room, or some times the dining room. Both are ideal choices for outdoor room extensions, as a small balcony could offer a superb plant display while a larger area could be furnished in the same style as the main room. Hi-tech, cottage chintz or a slick city look all are possible styles to consider.

The outdoor dining area

Installing a table and chairs will make eating outdoors, possibly with the prospect of spectacular urban or country views, irresistible. If you enjoy entertaining and plan to use your balcony as an outdoor dining room, you will want to take especial care to create the right ambiance. The furniture should be more comfortable than basic garden chairs so your diners will be encouraged to linger, but if you must make do with your existing utilitarian chairs, you can always dress them up for special occasions with tie-on cushions made from an appropriate fabric. Not only can they be matched to your table linen or a party theme, but they are also easily removed for cleaning or bringing indoors at the end of the day. Choosing and using balcony furniture is covered in more detail in Chapter Five.

Finding the right lighting

Dinner parties will require some form of lighting, unless a mid-city location provides its own illumination; candles are delightful but they do tend to flicker outdoors and can also attract a variety of insects. You could enclose your candles in special lanterns or glass jars; alternatively, if you plan to use the balcony often, it may be worth planning and installing a proper outdoor lighting system. Different types of lamp or spotlight can be concealed overhead, attached to walls and screens or hidden within the plant foliage to cast well-diffused light and interesting shadows. Some forms of garden lamp are more decorative and can be treated as accessories as well as a practical means of seeing what you are eating. The range of lighting available, and advice on installation, are included in Chapter Four.

Cooking al fresco

Dedicated al fresco diners like to cook on their balconies as well as eat there and will find room for a barbecue. Unless it is very large and sturdily built, the balcony may not be suited to one of the brick or stone built-in types of barbecue, which are efficient, convenient, good space-savers and almost obligatory for classic walled or concreted Mediterranean balconies or roof terraces. However, there are a great many lightweight free-standing barbecues that take up hardly any

A tiny kitchen balcony with scant room even for growing any edibles. However, the owners were determined to find space for enjoying the occasional al fresco meal with ever-changing views of river and city traffic.

space and which can be folded and put away at the end of the season.

Whatever type you choose, it is important to select a model and size that is suited to your needs – it is no fun catering for ten on a grill designed to feed two. Whether you choose to fuel it on charcoal (messy) or bottled gas (heavy to carry upstairs) will be determined by personal taste and practical considerations. When you have chosen your barbecue, you should make sure you know how to operate it properly. This is not just for safety reasons (a fire extinguisher on the balcony should be obligatory) but to save your own frustration and that of your neighbours.

STYLE AND SUITABILITY

Of course, choosing the right facilities to suit your home and lifestyle are important when planning and equipping a balcony, but it is equally important to select the correct features if you want them to be in keeping with the interior of your home and, often, the countryside or vista beyond. You should make the most of a view if you are lucky enough to have one, using plants and screens to frame rather than hide it, and choosing accessories to enhance the effect. For example, you should choose a style to reflect the shimmering heat and strong earthy colours if you are in the Mediterranean, the relaxed coolness and clear light in a seaboard location or the uncompromising hard lines and shiny edges of the big city.

If privacy and shelter are lacking, you can create window-like spaces and gaps in the trellis and climbing plants through which to enjoy the view without being one yourself. You might prefer to screen your balcony totally from the outside world, especially if you are faced with an eyesore or wish to create an escape from rather more mundane surroundings. All things are possible and you are limited only by your imagination. Since a balcony is approached only through the privacy of your home – and sometimes by an outdoor staircase from the garden – you can explore any theme and create any style and atmosphere you like with the right plants and accessories. Many people use their balconies as an excuse to indulge their favourite fantasy, with the total look and atmosphere often being adapted and extended from the style of the adjoining interior for most successful results.

Stained glass doors provide elegant access to a beautifully planted and well-screened roof garden used as a sunny extension to the sitting room and the perfect place to take tea on sunny afternoons.

31

CREATING A MEDITERRANEAN ATMOSPHERE

Even if you live in a chilly, grey climate it is possible to generate a sultry Mediterranean look with the help of plants with soft grey and scented foliage. *Euphorbia*, *Helichrysum* and *Artemisia* are all suitable, and hardy herbs such as sage, thyme and rosemary, all rich in aromatic oils, will release a wonderful scent when the sun shines on them or after a shower of rain. Exotically flowered climbers, such as the passion flower, *Passiflora*, or one of the more spectacular clematis could clothe your trellis and side partitioning. As a contrast, small clipped evergreens in formal geometric topiary shapes look well in pots and are easily positioned singly or in groups as living accessories.

Of course, if the balcony's microclimate permits, you can create a really authentic atmosphere with a collection of cacti, a rampant bougainvillaea, the beautiful oleander, *Nerium oleander* or one of the *Cistus*, or rock rose, family. If your balcony can take the weight, lots of terracotta pots and urns, with tiles on the floor and walls, will help to reinforce the look, as will, on frost-free balconies, richly patterned ceramic tiles from Spain, Portugal and Mexico. These can be used to great effect, not just as a flooring material but also as murals on walls and screening frames, or even as a tough but attractive table top. Add a brightly coloured awning or giant canvas sun umbrella, plus continental-style garden furniture, to maintain the right atmosphere.

CREATING A LUSH JUNGLE

Careful choice of dramatic foliage plants and possibly exotic flowers can transform a sheltered balcony into a wonderful jungle or sub-tropical extravaganza of bold leaf shapes and brightly coloured blooms. Some exciting species with oversized or interesting leaf forms are surprisingly hardy: *Fatsia japonica*, with its large hand-shaped leaves, and the spiky *Yucca filamentosa*, both grow well in pots and containers. Other good container foliage plants for the cooler balcony include ferns – from the large-leaved royal fern, *Osmunda regalis*, and waving ostrich feather fern, *Matteuccia struthiopteris*, to the delicate *Adiantum venustum* –

and fascinating hostas, whose leaves are thick and pleated in gold, blue and green. For contrast, there are many grasses which can be grown in tubs or pots: you could choose the vigorous gardener's garters (*Phalaris arundinacea* var. *picta*) or, if the container is a large one, the giant *Miscanthus sacchariflorus*. The luxury of a warm climate or sub-tropical conditions widens the scope to include the lush castor oil plant, *Ricinus communis*, a beautiful flowering hibiscus or the gloriously scented climber *Stephanotis floribunda*.

Cane or rattan furniture will reinforce the colonial or jungle atmosphere. Some people like to add fun accessories such as a wild animal sculpture or ornament lurking in the undergrowth, or ethnic touches, like primitive carvings and brightly coloured rugs as temporary screens or seating. Even a parrot in a cage might be considered the ideal finishing touch to such a scheme – a delightful fantasy perfect for a balcony opening off a bathroom or living room. This is a scheme that lends itself particularly well to being lit at night, with concealed upward-shining spotlights emphasizing the dramatic nature of the leaves to make a wonderful wild tableau.

CREATING AN ORIENTAL LOOK

For many, particularly city dwellers, the controlled minimalism and almost neutral colour schemes of classic oriental style is the perfect antidote to a stressful lifestyle and one which can be adopted right through the home. There is no reason why the balcony should not reflect an oriental mood too, particularly if it matches the style of the rest of the rooms, and this can be a very stylish and modern treatment despite being rooted in a classical philosophy and centuries-old design style.

Timber decking underfoot could be built on different levels, providing shelving or staging for a small stone bowl of water, a display of miniature bonsai trees in their attractive glazed bowls and dishes, or oriental-style ornaments and sculptures. The timber can be stained a soft blue or grey to increase the calm impression of peace and space, and extended to create screens and pergolas. For a more dramatic look, a Chinese red stain with touches of black can be used, maybe on the furniture and accessories. More subtle bamboo screens are also available, and are especially suited to

balconies as they are lightweight yet act as excellent screens and windbreaks.

Plants are kept to a minimum in the oriental scheme, each specimen being specially chosen for its shape and form. Bamboos are particularly appropriate, of course, are elegant and well suited to being grown in pots. The *Arundinaria* family can offer a wide range of delicate fluttering forms, from the hardy dark green *A. japonica* to the lovely golden leafed bamboo, *A. viridistriata* or purple-green *A. nitida*. They can look superb in a suitably oriental pot or urn. Other plants worth considering for an oriental-style balcony include a specimen dwarf maple, *Acer palmatum* which, with its lovely foliage and wonderful autumn colour, is suitable for a large container; and background greenery, preferably ever-green climbers and clipped forms. If the balcony is well supported, sculptural rocks and arrangements of pebbles can add to the authentic oriental feel and help to produce an excellent tranquil setting that looks good whatever the weather or time of year.

HIGH-TECH OR CITY STYLE

Similar, but without the oriental angle, is the high-tech or smart city look. Here the balcony might feature lots of clean timber or metal surfaces and structures, strong angular shapes and a limited colour scheme, especially in the choice of plants, to create a sophisticated, easily controlled and maintained outdoor area. An all-green theme is suitably restful if you lead a highly stressful life and, if you use evergreen plants, it will have year-round appeal. Alternatively, you could add a single secondary colour. White is a popular choice, or you could have cream for a softer feel; either can be adapted to flowers, variegated foliage, furniture and accessories for the completely co-ordinated look. There are lots of smart tricks you can play with colour, just as you would when planning an interior scheme: the occasional splash of red in a flower or accessory for example; a blend of pastel shades combining some of the newly developed flower shades or timber stains with furniture styles; or an unusual mix of blues and mauves – the possibilities are endless if you are prepared to sit down and plan exactly the look you want.

The clean lines of the modern balcony softened by curves and an overhead lattice which produces a pleasant dappled shade. Large pots of leafy plants flourish in the uninterrupted light and sunshine, providing life and interest on what is little more than an elevated walkway.

COUNTRY COTTAGE STYLE

Unlikely as it may seem, some people like to recreate an English country cottage atmosphere on their balconies. Nevertheless, it is perfectly possible, even in the tiniest area or mid-city location, if you have the right choice of plants and features: rambling roses; honeysuckle and ivies, for winter interest, climbing a rustic trellis; herbs and classic cottage plants planted in free-flowering groups in wooden tubs and suitably cottage-style containers.

This is a balcony that smells as sweet as it looks with carnations, stocks and the scent of herbs and flowering climbers. Spring brings tubs of hyacinths, delicately scented narcissi and wallflowers before they die back to be replaced with a multi-coloured show of bedding plants. For true authenticity, there should be a few edible plants such as strawberries, tomatoes, and maybe the odd lettuce or two, among the more ornamental plants. To sit and enjoy the experience, a classic wooden bench or a canvas deck-chair would be ideal.

The rambling, rather wild look of the country garden could also be tidied up slightly into a more formal style for a balcony, perhaps suiting a Georgian-style or particularly elegantly furnished home. You can buy stained or painted trellis work in all manner of formal styles, outdoor furniture smart enough to put in your dining room and sophisticated fibreglass plant containers that are both attractive and light-weight. With a well chosen piece of sculpture, a collection of evergreen topiary shapes in matching pots and a restrained planting scheme providing interest through the seasons, you can create an oasis of good taste and calm above the busiest street or screened from the gloomiest outlook.

UP ON THE ROOF

It is not much of a step from the balcony on to the roof, and in many ways a roof garden offers similar restrictions and benefits. Your property might even incorporate a kind of halfway hybrid – an outdoor patio area created on the flat roof of a single storey extension and accessible from one of the upper rooms. In many ways a balcony is a far more convenient and enjoyable facility than a roof garden, because access is easier and being able to walk into the room inside is undeniably a great advantage. Also, although a balcony is prone to high winds and weather extremes, it does not suffer quite as badly from these as a roof garden, which generally requires expert planning and a substantial form of screening if the area is to be successfully developed and planted, and its magnificent view is to be appreciated. On the plus side, a roof garden will normally offer more space to play with and thus more scope for your plans. Some owners are lucky enough to be able to create a whole garden, complete with lawns, trees and flower borders, but this requires time, money and a roof with excellent load-bearing properties. The majority of ideas and solutions in this book can be applied equally well to roof gardens providing you take into account their more stringent limitations.

CHAPTER THREE

PRACTICALLY PERFECT

LIMITATIONS AND LIABILITIES

Planning and designing a balcony area is an exciting prospect, but it is also something of a challenge even to the experienced garden designer or landscape architect. Apart from the obvious limitations of size and access, which are generally relatively easy to overcome given a little imagination and forethought, the elevated position and method of construction of balconies causes other problems. For example, their ability to take the weight of people, plants and other features should be questioned, and having the load-bearing capacity of your balcony checked by a professional should be your first prerogative. There are also other inherent problems which will have to be considered and resolved, such as exposure to extremes of weather, privacy where required and general safety, before you can contemplate the more pleasurable questions to be answered about designing and furnishing the area.

TAKING THE STRAIN

Many balconies, especially the more modern types which have become a vital element of the high-rise apartment block, and the majority of substantial upper storey patios and terraces found in hotter climates, were designed especially to

A plain wall or screen can be extended using lightweight bamboo or trellis for extra protection. Tubs of leafy plants and climbers are an effective and delightful disguise.

be used and furnished as a kind of outdoor living area. They are structurally supported and intended to take the weight of furniture and fittings, as well as all the popular *al fresco* activities such as eating and relaxing.

That said, it would be a good idea to explain your future plans and proposals to a qualified builder or architect and to make sure the structure is thoroughly checked and put in good repair. This is particularly important with balconies on older, often period, buildings where unseen timber and metal decay could give you expensive and potentially dangerous problems. Smaller balconies tend to be supported by a simple system of joists which may be capable of taking a fair amount of weight when in a good state of repair, but which are prone to damage from the weather and general fatigue and will require regular maintenance. It is advisable to be aware of any such defects right from the start, and to calculate the cost of strengthening or shoring up any major balcony defects in the earliest planning days so you can assess how much the restoration work will cost you. It may well be that the necessary work would be too difficult, too expensive or even that the proposed major changes would not be permitted because the property is listed as having a particular historical

Railings aren't simply a highly decorative and interesting architectural device. They are also an important safety feature to restrain plants and people.

importance. Any alterations may also contravene some lease agreements, so it would be wise to check out the legal implications too.

Then there are the smallest balconies of all: a decorative wrought iron grille, stone shelf or large ornamental timber box with just enough space for a single plant display. Some of them were not even designed for plants but were incorporated as an ornamental device in themselves, although the tendency these days is to add some bright display of seasonal blooms or a little trailing greenery. Once again, it would be as well to check the safety and strength of such tiny balconies – a medium-sized container of damp soil and a few plants can be surprisingly heavy and maybe weigh over 9 kg (20 lb).

Keeping the weight down

Whatever size and strength of balcony you have at your disposal, it makes sense to keep added weight to a minimum. It is best to consider the lighter flooring materials, for instance, such as timber, tiles and lightweight pavers rather than heavy concrete or stone slabs. Screens and partitions must be light but durable and flexible if they are to stand up to strong winds and the weight of climbing plants. Timber trellis comes in a great many styles and designs (see Chapter Four), or you could choose between metal mesh, plastic and bamboo types. If possible, you should also choose lightweight plant containers made of timber or fibreglass – the latter material has the advantage of being strong, light and available in a wide range of styles that imitate other, heavier materials. The weight of planting compost varies widely too, but the lighter, soil-less types contain a percentage of man-made material such as Perlite or Vermiculite, which also encourage good drainage.

Catching the drips

On the subject of drainage and water run-off, you should provide matching saucers or troughs for all your plant containers if you don't want to ruin your balcony floor (and the wall below) through spills and overflows. You should take particular care that saucers are attached to any pots or boxes attached to the front of the balcony or you will be

Stylish treatment for a dull back wall: ornamental trellis has been dramatically painted and the area floored to match internal decorations, creating a convincing indoor/outdoor environment. Raising the seating area slightly by means of shallow steps to make a kind of dais has increased the impression of privacy and privilege.

showering any passers-by below as well as ruining the fabric of the building. It is important that these trays and saucers are not too deep as otherwise they will collect lots of standing water which will tend to go stagnant.

To deal with rain-water, most balconies incorporate some form of integral drainage system that takes the water away through purpose-built drains rather than allowing it to run over the edge. However, they may need modifying or repairing, or you may have to adjust your plans so they do not interfere with the drainage system.

Protecting plants and furniture from the wind

When choosing your plants and containers, there can be a disadvantage in using lightweight pots and soil – large plants can topple over and you may have to compromise. Keeping the soil reasonably moist at all times will help to stabilize the pots. It is also a good idea to anchor all containers in some way – particularly those near the edge of the balcony or raised on shelves or ledges – so the weight of the plant or a gust of wind does not blow them over. The same rule applies to any furniture you choose for the balcony. Plastic, tubular metal and some wooden items are lightest but may also tend to blow over, so they should be firmly secured. If this is a problem, built-in furniture may be the answer; it will also save precious space.

Simple shelving on different levels and the use of large specimen plants have provided excellent shelter and privacy for this tiny area.

SAFETY FIRST

A balcony in a dangerous structural condition is a risk both to the user and to anyone unlucky enough to be passing underneath. Even a fragment of the structure or a stray railing could cause considerable, even fatal, damage to people or property below. The idea of the whole structure coming away from the wall doesn't bear thinking about, but if the building has been generally neglected, the ravages of time and exposure to extreme weather conditions make this a frightening possibility. You may need to support the balcony on sturdy metal props until the necessary restoration work can be completed.

Safeguarding against the weather

Other safety aspects should also be considered if you are a balcony owner. You have a responsibility to make sure that all fixtures, fittings, furniture and plant containers are well secured with no likelihood of them being knocked or blown off. This applies particularly to plant containers, especially if the plant is heavy and the pot light. Accidents are usually caused either through insufficient fixing to the balcony, or to extreme weather conditions such as the buffeting effect of prevailing winds or the unbalancing weight of snow. Window boxes, which are often fixed to the front of the balcony, and hanging baskets are particularly risky; they should be attached as securely as possible and their fixings checked at least once a year for wear and damage. Balancing pots (whether small or large) on a parapet or balustrade is not recommended unless you can guarantee there is no way they could be blown over or knocked off their perches by people or animals.

Checking railings and balustrades

There is also a risk of people falling off a balcony if the railings or balustrades are not adequate. In older properties these tend to get rather rickety and should be checked and restored if the balcony will be used regularly. You should never assume that no one will be putting them under any strain so they'll do for the present – it is a natural human response to lean over or against any type of railing. If you want to fix some kind of plant container to a railing, that is all the more reason to check its stability. If you need to repair or replace part or all of a railing or barrier, you will have to match it to the original style, more for the benefit of its external appearance than for your personal appreciation and satisfaction. In most cases this will involve a custom-made commission, often to a craftsman skilled in working with the appropriate metal, stone or ornamental timber if you want a well-matched repair or something in keeping with the balcony and the rest of the building.

Different styles

The style may vary according to local tradition or the quirks of the original architect. Low walls or balustrades in concrete or stone are not uncommon and brick is a possibility, either in a solid and often sweeping low wall or parapet, or ornamentally carved and shaped into a formal balustrade that affords views through as well as over the structure. Metal railings might be plain and straight or wrought into fantastic curly shapes and figures. They are almost always painted black, but sometimes they are white and matched to window shutters, a trellis or other surrounding architectural features.

Timber offers an equally wide range of options: straight up and down spindles may be square or rounded, and the balcony frontage may be close-boarded or incorporating

Because plants above ground level are exposed to strong winds and other extremes of weather, containers must be firmly secured and plants, especially climbers, well supported.

decorative shapes, cut-outs and carvings. Timber also lends itself to many different finishes, such as stains and varnishes, as well as flat paint and painted patterns and designs. Sometimes panels of toughened glass or plastic are used as an effective see-through barrier – usually when the property is sited by the sea to give an uninterrupted view of the beach and seascape. Ideally, these ornamental and practical barriers should be at least waist-height for safety, but in reality they may only reach an adult's knees – hardly reassuring or practical to the user.

If you feel the existing wall or railings are too low for your liking, you can increase their height with a section of firmly fixed trellis, metal or mesh or glass screening in a complementary style and colour. Alternatively, some balcony owners resolve the problem by placing stout boxes or containers of shrubby plants near the edge. However, building or lease restrictions may not allow this so it is advisable to check first. If that is the case, you may have to consider not using the balcony at all if it is small, designing it rather as an attractive backdrop, or positioning the 'living' area well to the back of the balcony if it is large enough.

PROTECTION AND PRIVACY

Because balconies extend beyond the protection of their main buildings and can be at any height, especially in the case of high-rise blocks, one of their worst drawbacks is being prone to exposure from the most severe weather conditions. High up, a biting wind is the worst enemy to balconies, not just because it causes damage but also because of the chill and dust that come with it. The unrelieved effects of strong sunshine and winter weather can be equally damaging.

Screening out the weather

In countries where the summers are hot, even a first storey balcony can suffer terribly from the bleaching and weathering results of the sun. An unshaded sun-trap is not quite the asset it may at first seem when it is simply too hot to sit outside comfortably and all the plants quickly shrivel up and die. There is also the terrible blistering and destruction of the actual fabric of the balcony and its features to be considered. Some form of protection is essential in almost all

Sliding glass doors are an ideal means of enjoying the elevated garden from indoors whatever the weather, especially when the aspect is as well planted as this one.

Before starting any work you will need to check the condition of the basic structure and budget for any necessary restoration.

cases if the balcony is to be comfortable to use and the plants and features are to survive.

Screening should be erected where appropriate to protect the area from scorching sunshine and also from prevailing winds. Broken screening is more effective than the solid variety: its natural flexibility enables it to stand up much better to storm-force gales, while dappled shade is far more attractive than dense gloom even when the weather is unbearably hot.

Overhead shelter

Some form of overhead shelter is frequently necessary, and it may be worth considering a permanent roof structure in cold or wet climates if one is not already incorporated since anything less would be unable to bear the weight of regular snowfalls. A fabric awning, overhead trellis or pergola threaded with plants, temporary sheeting or bamboo matting, or even a large continental-style umbrella, are all good sun screens and suit most tastes and styles.

Decorative ideas

Some forms of screening are more decorative than others – you will find ornamental trellis and screens discussed in Chapter Four, as well as the wonderful variety of climbing plants that can be used to clothe them, rather in the way that curtains enhance a window in an interior scheme. More basic, practical forms of screening may be made from timber, perspex or metal mesh, bamboo, rustic poles or plastic-coated wire. You can even use stretched canvas or other sun-proof fabrics as a seasonal screen. In the right position they can serve their purpose well and the most basic forms may be already fitted when you take possession of your balcony. If they are not decorative enough for your taste, they can always be dressed up slightly or even transformed, using paint, timber stains or climbing plants. If you are using perspex, however, it will accept none of these treatments although its transparent nature is an advantage if you want protection without losing your view. The alternative is to erect a secondary, more decorative screen in front of the practical, less attractive version; this is a useful option if you are not permitted to make any permanent structural alterations on the balcony.

Providing privacy

On many balconies, screening serves another, almost equally important practical purpose – that of providing privacy. The balcony is naturally a private place: it is part of your home, reached only through one of your rooms, and generally strongly reflects your personal taste and lifestyle. It is a place for escape and relaxation. Railings or a low parapet are usually adequate at the front, especially if the balcony is high up, since you are unlikely to be viewed from ground level.

The shared balcony is a different matter – the type where a continuous structure provides facilities for a whole row of apartments. In this case some substantial form of side screening is necessary. You may also have to screen the area from above to avoid a neighbour's prying gaze or friendly interference. Any of the more substantial decorative screening ideas would be adequate, particularly when clothed in climbing plants, which are one of the best screening devices of all. Remember, though, that if you want to maintain your privacy right through the seasons, you should choose evergreen species for your climbers.

Sliding glass doors may provide an excellent uninterrupted view but they will need some form of screening on cold nights or over-bright days. Vertical or horizontal slatted blinds are among the most popular and successful practical but decorative solutions.

LEGAL RESTRICTIONS

An important point already touched upon, but which you may not have considered, is the possible legal limitations of owning a balcony. In an apartment block there are often restrictions controlling the external appearance of the building; you may not be allowed to make any structural or even semi-permanent additions and so may have to rely on arrangements of plants for all your screening and decorative effects instead. In London's new Docklands development apartments, for example, those occupants with a balcony overhanging the Thames are subject to a heavy annual surcharge imposed under regulations governing the use of the river. The pleasure of watching boats and other river traffic pass by can be as costly as having your own mooring. Even if you don't live at such a prestigious address it is wise to check your lease or local planning restrictions before making any major changes to your balcony.

INSIDE OUT

To get the maximum and best use from your balcony, you should consider very carefully the link between it and your home. On a practical level, access must be suited to the way in which you will use the area: do you want sliding glass doors or windows that turn it into an extension of the main room, or a single door or pair of elegant french windows that encourage you to step outside? The advantage of choosing patio windows is that they transform the well-planned balcony into a spectacular tableau even during the colder months or, with the addition of lighting, into a splendid backdrop at night. The other advantage of the plate-glass effect is that it can create a wonderful impression of space, especially if the flooring material – such as timber or tiles – matches that of the room inside. To encourage this impression further you could also choose a similar style of furniture and colour theme, and place plenty of large leafy houseplants close to the door or window so it is hard to see where one mass of greenery ends and the other begins. Plate glass and patio doors certainly give a wonderful, uninterrupted view. However, they do not always suit a traditional interior where an elegant glass door or pair of french windows will be far more in keeping, yet still offer adequate access to the balcony.

Care should be taken to ensure that both the basic structure and any overhanging boxes are in good condition and securely attached.

Curtain treatments

You will not want a view of the balcony all the time: during the day the light may be too bright, or you may wish to shut out the night for warmth, privacy or a sense of security, so some form of internal screening will be necessary. How you decide to screen the window or door will depend on your interior furnishings, of course. If they are traditional, floor-length curtains can frame and emphasize a fine door and may match the other soft furnishings in the room. Alternatively, the curtains may run across most or all of the wall, and be used to disguise it when closed. The curtain treatment itself can be as simple or as elaborate as you like, maybe with a deep ornate pelmet or simply hung from a brass or wooden pole. Tie-backs of some kind are a good way of holding the curtains to either side of the window (or one side if you opt for the very stylish look of a single generous curtain sweeping a handsome french window or door). They can be made in matching or contrasting fabric, in the shape of lined or edged bands or giant bows, or take the form of fat colour co-ordinated tassels, looped on to special hooks or metal cleats fixed to the wall. Alternatively, you can simply hook the curtains behind a round wooden or metal device which also fastens to the wall.

Using blinds

Large patio doors and extensive areas of glass are more difficult to dress and screen attractively, especially if you are aiming at something stunning or eye-catching with a modern feel to it. You can use curtains, of course, but if such a large expanse of fabric is undesirable (or too expensive, because the fabric will have to be at least twice the width of the window to allow for gathers) blinds are by far the best and most practical alternative. Venetian blinds are particularly attractive when used in this way and offer excellent flexibility, allowing the window or door to be totally or partially screened as well as left completely uncovered. The dappled shade which is produced by partly opening the slats can be really lovely.

Blinds are usually made to measure and come in a wide choice of slat widths – the narrow types are the most stylish – and virtually every colour imaginable from pastels and strong primaries to smart metallic shades. This is a treatment that looks as good from outside as it does indoors – another point worth considering when planning your windows. Also popular for patio windows are vertical blinds which offer the same flexibility in use but have a more limited choice of colours. They may not be as attractive as venetian blinds, unless you can find a style with relatively narrow slats, but they are less expensive to buy. For a very natural effect that may suit a predominance of natural timber in your scheme, both indoors and out, and the proximity of lots of leafy plants, you can buy tiny slatted wooden blinds, called pinoleum blinds, which look very attractive in the right setting. You can also buy natural cane, bamboo and reed roller blinds which look particularly good when used to echo an oriental or softly neutral theme.

Strong canvas attached to metal frames is a quick and useful way to create additional privacy and shelter from side draughts.

CHAPTER FOUR

FIXTURES AND FITTINGS

FLOORS, WALLS AND STRUCTURAL FEATURES

Like bathrooms, kitchens and other characteristically small interior rooms, it pays to design and install major permanent features carefully if space is limited. As with any stylish but hard-working living area, the balcony requires a tough but decorative flooring, well-planned facilities, perhaps for cooking and dining, plus an effective, attractive means of providing shade and shelter. Special areas for storage, seating and plant display, built into the design, may also be needed.

A balcony imposes even more restrictions than a patio, all of which must be strictly observed if it is to be designed and used successfully. Not only must it withstand the prevailing weather conditions, as we discussed in Chapter Three, but you must also choose materials and features that are reasonably lightweight or at least within the load-bearing abilities of the main structure, while blending harmoniously with the rest of the building. Limited access to many balconies can cause additional problems in the early stages of refurbishment, especially when installing large, bulky or messy building materials. You will also have to bear this in mind when selecting such items as timber, paving slabs or concrete. Panels of trellis or screening often have to be purchased in small sections so they can be reassembled, or the whole structure built from scratch, *in situ*, because otherwise they will be too awkward to be taken through the

Patterned walling blocks make an unusual and practical broken screen for climbing and foliage plants with a green/white theme.

house or apartment, or too large to go through the doors opening on to the balcony. It may be possible to winch or lift large and awkward materials up to the balcony from outside, but you should remember that hiring the relevant equipment will add considerably to the cost and work of the total project.

DECORATIVE SCREENING

Your first consideration will probably be the style and type of screening that is going to give the balcony shelter and a modicum of privacy. In a block of apartments some form of partition or screening between you and your neighbours is often already in place, but it is rarely adequate and even less likely to be aesthetically pleasing or suited to your design plans. It may be a very basic metal or reinforced glass partition or, at best, a low stretch of decorative wrought ironwork which may look attractive and complement the style and construction of the balcony, but which has no practical purpose other than establishing your boundaries. It is often written into the lease on a property that these partitions must not be removed or structurally altered, so if you don't like them you will have to disguise them in some way. If you can spare the space, you could always erect your preferred form of screening in front of the original one. However, do remember that whatever you choose for the balcony must combine good looks and strength without weighing too much, so brick or stone screens are usually out of the question, unless you construct a lightweight partition and use facing versions of these materials.

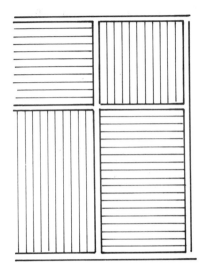

Light but offering good wind resistance, louvred panels create an attractive dappled shade. They look particularly good when different sizes and patterns are combined.

Disguising existing screens

If an existing screen is high enough, it may be tempting to think you can simply disguise it with the help of a vigorous evergreen climber, such as an ivy, planted in a large pot or tub. Unfortunately that is not possible if the panels are made from glass, perspex or metal as the plants will have nothing to cling to as they climb. The best space-saving solution here is to construct thin trellis-work, made from plastic, metal or timber, to cover the screen and for the plants to clamber over. If you choose a trellis that looks reasonably attractive, or perhaps install it on the diagonal rather than in a conventional grid pattern, you will immediately improve the look of the area even before the plants have had a chance to establish themselves. Alternatively, you could hang a selection of trailing and flowering plants from the trellis-work in light plastic pots (a piece of wire around the rim or piercing the top of the pot should serve as an adequate hook) as a temporary and extremely effective instant display, while more permanent specimens are growing.

Another idea worth considering as a cunning and eye-deceiving disguise is to paint the support. Paint it white if you want it to look light and attract the eye, black or dark brown for drama, or a deep green or blue for a more sophisticated effect. You may even be bold enough to experiment with rich reds and russets if you are planning an oriental-style balcony or something slightly unusual. If you want an inexpensive and easy alternative – perhaps if you are not planning to stay in residence long, or the property is only rented so you are not able to make major alterations and additions – it might be possible to use the wire or plastic mesh designed for plant support. You can buy it quite cheaply in rolls or sheets and then fling it over and fix it round the partition. You would have to attach it very firmly, especially if the site is exposed to strong winds, but it does have the advantage of being extremely light.

You should also bear in mind that mature climbing plants can be surprisingly heavy, especially the flowering shrub types, so in this case it might be better to choose one of the smaller climbers and clingers such as a small-leaved ivy. Better still, particularly if you want a quick, temporary effect for the summer months only, grow a pretty annual climbing plant, such as a sweet pea (*Lathyrus odoratus*) or morning glory (*Ipomoea*) which will smother your netting with beautiful foliage and flowers in a single season.

Disguising the main wall

While you are considering disguises and cover-ups, spare a thought for the rear wall of the balcony – the main wall of the property. A balcony may feel like a three-sided feature, but when you are sitting in it, that fourth surface is visually very important, and may also be visible from below. Most likely to be made from brick or stone, it is not always very attractive, especially when the balcony is sited at the rear of the building, and may also need a little cosmetic treatment

to make it blend in with the style and atmosphere of your balcony plans. This can be more important in the case of a small balcony than with a large one, when you might at least have room to stand tubs of tall plants against the wall. All the same, you can use the same cover-up tricks as you did for the side partitions, but here you have the advantage of a much sturdier, stronger surface to work on because it is the main load-bearing wall of the property. However, you should still check that the basic construction is sound and in good decorative order, and carry out any necessary repairs such as repointing or repainting before you cover it up.

INTERNAL PARTITIONS

On larger balconies it may be desirable to erect some form of internal partitioning, using the more decorative forms of trellis. This might be to separate one part of the balcony from another: perhaps to enclose a small dining or hot tub area, to provide extra shelter or privacy, or to create a more intimate atmosphere. Whether you opt for an internal screen, back wall cover-up or important side shelter, the scope and range of trellisage and screens are almost infinite.

The use of timber by modern landscapers and architectural designers has been particularly exciting, drawing on classical themes as well as creating eye-catching new designs. The simple principle of interlocked or woven slats seems to offer an infinite variety of patterns. They can be laid straight in a checkered design, or, more stylishly, on the diagonal or even simply constructed in vertical parallels. Struts can be flat and wide or slim and narrow to vary the effect and the profile can be curved or angular, arched or pyramid-shaped. Some of the most exciting effects incorporate more than one of these ideas in panels or sections to create a complete and much more complex design. Some trellises have two layers for maximum protection, while others incorporate windows through which to appreciate a view. Particularly effective, and easily adapted to any size or shape, are small square sections of timber trellis, each incorporating a slightly

Extensive use of terracotta pots and pavers with a selection of dark green foliage plants and luxurious upholstered furniture creates an unmistakably Mediterranean atmosphere.

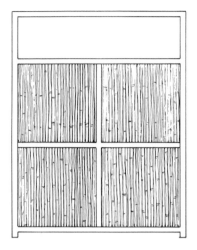

Panel screening may be infilled with louvred, bamboo or any natural woven material. Some areas may be left open for further decorative effect.

different design: arranged vertically, horizontally or including random spaces. A combination of different types fixed side by side can look very effective indeed, like a sophisticated kind of subtle patchwork producing lovely striped shadows. More lovely designs are inspired by such classical themes as the columns and arches of a Greek temple, a medieval scalloped profile, Georgian formality or ornamental Gothic posts and finials.

Timber screens

Timber is equally flexible in its size and finish too; it can be constructed to any height or assembled in sections to any width or shape that fits your balcony. These sections might be stained and varnished in the traditional wood shades of rich red, dark or honey brown, or given a softer, more weathered look or more up-to-date appearance with one of

Where protection but an uninterrupted view is required, reinforced glazed panels are sometimes erected within a sturdy frame.

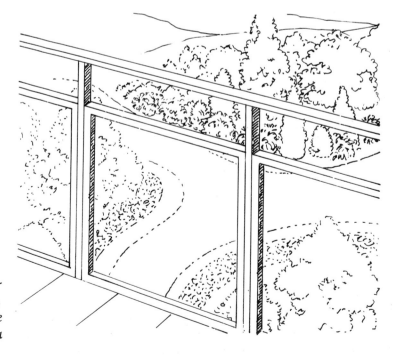

the new pastel-shaded stains – perhaps a soft grey or sea-bleached blue. For a more dramatic effect, the trellis might even be stained a smart dark green, deep blue or strong Chinese red. Timber can be as subtle or as stunning as you wish (remember that matt and satin varnishes are not as hard-edged and shiny as gloss paint); it can even have an unmistakably rustic air if you use simple chestnut poles nailed together to make a framework. For a very soft, natural look that is quick and easy to install, you can buy willow hurdles, bamboo or reed screens which are available in sections and simply fixed to a timber frame. They also make an excellent disguise for an existing wall or partition, providing an instant cover-up or temporary screen which is easily dismantled should you want to replan your balcony or move home. They look especially good in a modern or oriental scheme.

Metal screens

Metal is another exciting screening material if handled boldly. Meshed screens may offer a variety of patterns and designs, including cut-outs, and are easily spray-painted in your chosen colour – including shiny metallic finishes or glossy black for a really stunning hi-tech scheme. Alternatively, dramatic metal struts are sometimes erected as plant supports in pyramid or arched shapes, and then infilled with wires or netting.

Metal does have its softer, more traditional aspect too, and is also available as old-fashioned Victorian-style trellis sections, arches and frames, often used to create rose arbours and bowers. They are lightweight and are particularly suitable as plant supports if firmly fixed in place, or attached directly to the back wall to add interest.

OVERHEAD EFFECTS

Some form of overhead structure is frequently necessary, both for privacy and to create a pleasing sense of seclusion. It will also act as a shelter by filtering light summer showers or the debilitating effects of strong sunshine. A climbing plant produces the most natural effect and, if you choose a quick-growing annual or deciduous type, it will allow more light on to the area during the winter months. Climbing roses, clematis and wisteria are particularly suited to this treatment since they offer the dual advantage of attractive foliage and beautiful flowers in spring or summer.

Pergolas

The most usual form of support for plants – and it needs to be strong, even for slender twining annuals like sweet peas – is a series of metal wires or a pergola structure. A pergola is the most ornamental option and provides interest even through the winter months when it may be totally or partially uncovered because the plants have died back. It is also sturdy enough for lightweight canvas or bamboo screens to be pulled across it in particularly hot weather, or throughout the summer, if plants have not been chosen to smother the structure. Cane mats or reed panels can also be attached to the sides for screening and to produce a more enclosed, private area.

A pergola is usually made of timber, often rough-sawn, although it can be sanded and specially finished with paint or varnish for more sophisticated schemes. However, for a lighter effect, it could equally well be constructed using unpeeled larch poles, bamboo (fixed with galvanized nails but superficially bound with twine for a traditional oriental effect – space them closer to create more shading) or metal poles. For that chunky hi-tech look, you could even use steel girders, painted perhaps a dark grey, blue or ox-blood red.

A pergola is really little more than a simple framework with a series of crossbeams along the top; these are usually allowed to extend beyond the framework rather than being cut flush, for a more attractive appearance and to suspend hanging baskets from the overhang if wished. It needs to be well-supported, usually by a series of vertical supports, and firmly fixed to the back wall. For reasons of safety and security, it may also be necessary to add further support in the form of a tensioning cable attached to a nearby wall or similar firm structure. Metal wires are far less decorative but relatively unobtrusive if you prefer your climbing plants to take predominance. Stainless steel or plastic-covered wires should be properly spaced and stretched under tension to provide adequate and safe support.

Timber is a wonderfully versatile material and, being lightweight and adaptable, is ideal for creating custom-made flooring, screening and overhead shelter on both the modern or country-style roof garden. Here decking has been usefully extended to surround a hot tub.

OTHER SCREENING IDEAS

There are other options for providing shade and shelter to the well-designed balcony area. They may be a summer-only arrangement (but you will need somewhere to store them when not in use) or a more permanent structure which should be designed to stand up to all weathers, including high winds and the weight of snow and rain.

Awnings

Awnings can be adapted to all styles and schemes and are reasonably simple to erect on an overhead frame. For a bright continental effect, there are many ready-made and gaily striped awnings available, as well as those in floral and geometric patterned fabrics. Whichever style you choose, the material must be tough and specially recommended for use in strong sunshine, so the colours do not fade and the fabric does not rot easily. The designs could be matched to other furnishings on the balcony, such as the cushions, seat covers

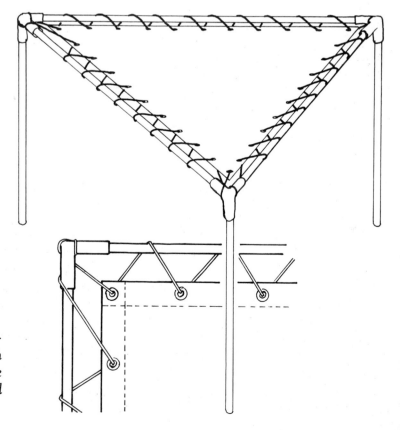

A free-standing overhead awning might be made from sailcloth tied to a tubular metal frame using strong nylon rope threaded through metal eye-holes.

and table cloths, or the fabric used to recover deckchairs or make side screens.

You can buy an automatic awning which is ideal for small balconies. It fixes on to the main wall of the building and can be drawn out or folded away as required. You can even buy an electrically operated option on some models which is controlled from inside the home. The more decorative awnings might include a scalloped edge or decorative trimming such as tassels or binding. For a more subtle effect, guaranteed to blend in with the surrounding plants and timber features, you can use bamboo or rush matting, stretched unbleached sailcloth or sacking, all of which can be designed to roll back over an overhead framework.

Umbrellas and parasols

One of the simplest and most convenient forms of shading and shelter, of course, is the good old sun umbrella or parasol. This is easily stored away when not in use yet can be erected instantly whenever it is needed. On the balcony it is important to make sure any umbrellas are stable, either by slotting them into a mounting hole in the centre of a garden table or providing a similar facility in your decking or paving. If this is not practical, you will have to consider a hollow plastic base, usually weighted with water or sand. There is a wide range of designs in umbrellas to match the upholstery on many patio furniture ranges, from stripes and florals to plain calico or canvas.

CREEPING AND CLIMBING PLANTS

There is such a wonderful variety of climbing and trailing plants that have decorative foliage, wonderful flowers and sometimes bright fruits too, that choosing just two or three for a balcony can be very difficult. Unless the area is a large one, you are unlikely to be able to choose more than a couple of plants. Your wall or screening will offer the protection and support they need to flourish and your final selection will be influenced not just by the prevailing climate in your area, but also by whether they will be in a protected sunny position or a colder, windy one. For example, save your camellia, honeysuckle and jasmine for decorating

One of the simplest but most stunning forms of overhead shelter is a giant fabric umbrella. As well as affording shade and privacy, it can be matched to upholstered furniture, table linen and other accessories.

north- and east-facing trellises, because a sunny aspect will better suit the lovely lilac-flowered wisteria or one of the vigorously flowering *Solanum* family.

Plants for quick cover

The majority of climbing plants shoot up so quickly they are a pleasure to grow – they will partly smother and soften a trellis or overhead structure within a single season. Many are also sweetly scented, so add another dimension to your balcony scheme. Luckily most will be happy if planted in a large pot, tub or container, provided they are given the right type of soil (some will not tolerate an alkaline compost) and are fed regularly to keep pace with their rapid growth. Some may need pruning or training into position, particularly if they threaten to cover a window, viewing gap or anywhere you don't want them to go. If you want year-round appeal, choose at least one evergreen climber. Ivies (*Hedera*) are available in a wide variety of leaf shapes and colours, including variegated effects, from the large-leaved Persian ivy, *H. colchica* to the many gold, cream or purple variegated forms of *H. helix*.

If you want a sophisticated predominance of greenery for a background you should look for climbers with interesting foliage shapes, such as the quick-growing golden hop, *Humulus lupulus* 'Aureus', or one of the large-leaved *Actinidia* family, which are vigorous climbers ideal for covering large areas. You could choose *A. chinensis*, which produces edible fruits in the right conditions, or the more delicate *A. kolomikta* (sometimes called the 'cat-plant' as they seem to find the plant irresistible) which has the most beautiful pink colouring on the foliage in early summer.

Flowering climbers

It would be a shame not to have at least one flowering climber on the balcony. If you want a low-key, sophisticated look, you could choose the climbing hydrangea, *H. petiolaris*, which is useful for its hardiness, fine foliage and simple white blooms, or the exceedingly fast-growing Russian vine, *Polygonum baldschuanicum*, ideal for quick balcony cover and producing a froth of white flowers rather than spectacular individual blooms.

For a more dramatic look, few can resist growing one of the clematis species – a group which includes so many varieties you could have one in flower from very early spring to late autumn. Despite their often exotic blooms (especially the familiar large purple flowers of C. 'Jackmanii') there is an evergreen form, C. *armandii*, which has pretty pink/white flowers and the spectacular C. *montana*, which is a great cover-all and produces an absolute cloud of pink or white flowers. If you want something hardy but which looks exotic, *Clianthus puniceus* is an evergreen that produces clusters of bright red flowers, and there are both hardy and tender forms of the extraordinary passion flower, *Passiflora*. Strictly speaking, laburnum is not a climber, but it is a wonderful subject for a pergola or overhead structure through which the golden flowers will hang in long racemes.

Fruiting climbers

These should not be forgotten either – even if your balcony does not enjoy the type of climate that will ripen off the fruits, the majority of fruiting climbers are still worth growing for their attractive flowers and foliage. There are a great many members of the *Vitis* family, for example, which are purely ornamental vines and excellent balcony climbers, while V. *vinifera* includes several varieties that will produce edible grapes given the right conditions. You will find a wide choice of soft and hard fruits that can be trained up a wall or trellis mentioned in Chapter Two.

Annual climbers

For quick temporary effects, or to add variety each year, annual climbers are no less attractive. Because they grow particularly fast, they are useful for quick, almost instant cover, perhaps while you are waiting for a slower growing, more permanent climber to establish itself. The blue trumpet flowers of the morning glory, *Ipomoea rubrocaerulea*, make a wonderful display until they fade in the afternoon – a new crop of blooms appears the following morning. The climbing nasturtium, *Tropaeolum*, can also be relied on, this time for a continuous show of brilliant red and orange flowers. For scent and a long lasting display of delicate blooms, you can't beat the fast-growing sweet pea, *Lathyrus*, in shades of blue, pink, white, cream and mauve.

Sub-tropical climbers

Those fortunate enough to enjoy a climate capable of sustaining sub-tropical and more tender plant species have an even more exciting choice of climbers. You may be lucky enough to persuade mimosa (*Acacia dealbata*), that classic South of France and native Australian climber, to flower in cooler zones, but generally, although reasonably hardy, it requires a good hot summer to produce its distinctive fluffy yellow flowers with their strong scent the following spring. The silvery grey-green foliage is also attractive in its own right. Dutchman's pipe, *Aristolochia elegans*, is an excellent overhead climber, producing hanging purple blotched flowers, and *Mandevilla* × *amabilis* is a tropical twiner whose rose-coloured flowers open at night – an excellent choice if this is when you are most likely to use your balcony.

TAKE TO THE FLOOR

Your balcony may be strong enough to take the weight of the full range of patio paving materials, but it would probably not be advisable to use the heavier paving slabs and stone setts as they will put unnecessary stress on the structure. Some mild climates extend the flooring options into more decorative but tough materials, such as clay and ceramic tiles or decorative mosaics which might crack if subjected to frost. In between there are a great many attractive options, including individual paving units in different shapes and colours for creating bonds, weaves and herringbone patterns. You can combine different shapes and shades to form an almost infinite variety of designs. For the most stylish effect, you could match the balcony floor to that of the adjoining room, especially if you are using tiles or pavers, to create a superb feeling of continuity and space. A plate glass window or patio doors encourages the visual illusion.

Timber decking

One of the most popular balcony flooring materials, and one which adapts itself particularly well to indoors and out, is timber decking. It is lightweight and flexible, making it ideal from a practical point of view, and capable of being extended neatly into other built-in features, such as furniture and staging. Sections can be laid in all manner of decorative herringbone and ornamental patterns, and the timber stained and varnished or painted to create a natural or dramatic finish. Decking is available in ready-made sections which can be fitted together in any combination you wish, and which make an excellent portable flooring for temporary transformation of an existing, less attractive balcony floor.

If you are building your own decking, you can adapt it exactly to your needs, incorporating interesting changes of level, planters and other features. Hardwoods, such as redwood and red cedar, are ideal because they will not readily rot or warp. However, you can use softwoods like spruce and larch providing you are prepared to give them an annual treatment of preservative and an occasional stiff brushing to remove any slippery algae growth.

BUILT-IN FEATURES

Purpose-made features and furnishings make the most of limited space and can be a real boon to a small balcony. For example, you could have permanent bench seating (lift-up seats provide handy extra storage for garden implements, cushions and other items), with maybe a simple matching table for casual meals. The whole unit can either be neatly tucked into a corner or designed to create a central island unit, perhaps with raised bed facilities for growing plants between the seating too. Built-in plant boxes and containers are particularly useful positioned around the perimeter of the balcony or just along the front edge, and provide an additional safety feature. For the smartest effect, they can match your flooring or screening materials to encourage a sense of space and continuity. Alternatively, they can be faced with decorative bricks or tiles. On a larger balcony, such features could be usefully employed as area dividers or to enclose a small pool.

Shelves and low platforms are useful for displaying plants in pots, ornaments and sculpture, and can be adapted to whatever materials you have available and the shape and size of your balcony. A slab of stone, marble or timber mounted on bricks or blocks makes an excellent, easily assembled low plinth which doubles as a bench; or timber planks could be hung on chains or fastened directly to the back wall. Where screens or trellis are not strong enough to take the weight of

Lightweight trellis makes attractive internal partitioning, ideal for screening different areas even within a small space. Make the trellis as simple or elaborate as you want. You can also have decorative raised beds made of timber. Note the use of timber decking to introduce an attractive feel.

shelving, free-standing storage constructed in timber or metal will provide reliable facilities, but should be fastened down in some way to prevent strong winds getting behind or beneath it and toppling the whole thing over. If you have the space, some form of weatherproof built-in cupboard is exceedingly useful for storing soft furnishing items or fold-away furniture, as well as small gardening tools and maintenance equipment, at night or over the winter.

WAYS WITH WATER

If you take its limitations into consideration and adapt your ideas accordingly, all things are possible on a balcony. There is no reason why you should not incorporate a water feature in your plans. In fact, so long as it is carefully planned and sensibly installed, a small pool or moving water feature can be a real asset, giving life and sparkle to your scheme. The sound and sight of water also have wonderful relaxing qualities, so are particularly appropriate to this high-level retreat and antidote to executive living.

Considering the weight

The biggest problem, as usual, is weight; water weighs 4.5 kg (10 lb) for every 4.5 litres (1 gallon), and that does not include the weight of the container. However, one of the smaller features should be possible, even if it is only a head spouting water into a small bowl fixed to the back wall of the balcony. A small raised pool could be incorporated among your built-in features – a plastic liner faced in matching brick, timber or tiles. With the addition of a small underwater pump this could even include a modest fountain effect, or you could design two pools arranged on different levels, with one running into the other in a most soothing manner. Alternatively, you might buy one of the pre-formed (and lightweight) fibreglass pools, although you will have to disguise it in some way.

The simplest and quickest option is to create a miniature pool out of an old half-barrel or any waterproof plant container – it could be a glazed terracotta or stone urn, or even a plastic trough. This will be big enough for one or two interesting water plants, perhaps a miniature waterlily, or, if you prefer, a small bubble fountain or some small fish.

Moving water features

Small moving water features, operated by an electric pump and incorporating a hidden reservoir for recycling the water, are even more economical on weight and space. Water can be designed to cascade over a rock, a metal ball or collection of pebbles, or to spout out of a wall-mounted ornament. There are also free-standing water features such as fountains, urns and sculptures. With any moving water feature, it is important that you choose correctly for the size of pool or reservoir. Splashing and spillage could ruin your balcony and also mean you will have to keep topping up the water level.

BARBECUES

You can't beat the flavour of food cooked and eaten outdoors and there is a particular pleasure in the seclusion of the self-catering balcony. Barbecuing imparts a distinctive and delicious smoky flavour to grills and spit-roasted meats, and the technique can be used in cooking foil-wrapped vegetables and desserts with equally excellent results.

If you have the space, a built-in barbecue could be extended into a complete cooking and dining complex with serving counters, integrated shelves, cupboards and seating taking up surprisingly little space. Shelter from prevailing winds would be particularly important for comfort and efficiency; you might also like to install a permanent chimney to take away the smoke.

The alternative is a mobile barbecue which might be as simple as an open charcoal-fired grill on long legs, sometimes equipped with wheels so that you can move it easily. The more sophisticated models are electric or gas-powered, both of which may be a cleaner, safer option for high-rise cooking, and rely on heated lava rocks to impart that familiar smoky flavour. The disadvantage of a gas barbecue is storage and access to the gas bottles, but it does offer exact temperature control, instant lighting and various spit and oven features. An electric barbecue requires only a heavy-duty extension lead but there are few models from which to choose and they are more expensive to run.

Maximizing a minimal balcony with chain-slung shelving for plants and a quarry-tiled floor picking up the warm colour of natural terracotta pots. The primarily russet and green colour scheme prevents the general impression of profusion looking messy or confused.

BATHING

Those with only a small backyard or balcony at their disposal need not be envious of garden owners with their own private swimming pools. Hot tubs and spas can be just as much fun, take up the minimum of space and because the water is heated, can be used in any climate and at any time of the year. Their only drawback for balcony installation is the extreme weight of the tub and its water. With bathers, too, a standard hot tub could weigh up to 3628 kg (8000 lb). You will need a reinforced concrete slab 10–15 cm (4–6 in) thick to take the weight; alternatively, support it on reinforced concrete piers or wooden joists. A qualified builder or architect should be able to advise if this is practical.

Hot tubs

As their name suggests, hot tubs usually comprise a circular tub (although other shapes are available) made from a hardwood, such as redwood or cedar, that is resistant to moisture and free of splinters. It can be half-framed in a timber-decked platform for easy access and a neat built-in appearance, or left standing as it is on the balcony floor. Seats inside bring the warm water up to chin level and a system of heaters and jets keep it bubbling with a pleasant massaging sensation that is supposed to be an excellent antidote to stress.

Spas

Spas work on a simpler principle but are made of fibreglass so are lighter and less expensive to buy. However, they are not particularly attractive, so do need to be disguised in some way with a timber surround, or lots of plants in pots standing close by. Hot tubs and spas need good screening for privacy and shelter, overhead as well as around – it would be sensible to site one as close to the house as possible if you intend to use it in cold weather. Using plenty of leafy plants in boxes and containers will further encourage the sense of privacy and cosiness. You will also require access to a safe electricity supply for operating pumps and heaters, so do bear that in mind and plan accordingly. Again, an architect or builder should be able to advise you if you are in any doubt.

AFTER DARK

A properly designed and expertly installed outdoor lighting system is virtually essential to all but the smallest balcony. Having said that, even a tiny, plant-only display might benefit from being illuminated when viewed from the house or ground level, so its architectural charms can be highlighted and emphasized in relief, as well as produce leaf and flower shadows.

If your balcony is divided from your home by a large expanse of glass, you could rely on your room to illuminate the area, but this is not very exciting, nor as effective. Lighting not only transforms the balcony into a living tableau to be appreciated in comfort from indoors through plate glass in winter, or an open door in warmer weather, but it also means it can be used at night for relaxing or dining. As well as serving a practical purpose, outdoor lighting can be used to stunning decorative effect: spotlights highlighting the shape of statuary or architecturally foliaged plants, or downlighters making soft pools of light filtered through an overhead climbing plant or pergola structure. A well-planned combination of up- and downlighters produces a wonderful moonlight effect.

Installing the lighting

All light fitments used outdoors should be sturdy and well made and must be guaranteed waterproof. Unless you know exactly what you are doing, they should always be installed by a qualified electrician who can advise on how many lamps might be run from a single cable. If you are using low-voltage lights, there is also a limit to how many lights you can run through a single transformer, for example. The size of the cable and length it has to run will also affect performance and the number of lights it can handle.

All cables for exterior use should be protected by a special plastic conduit, which can be clipped out of sight along the balcony perimeters, maybe behind plant tubs or troughs, or attached to an overhead pergola structure and concealed by climbing plants. You should also insist on the system being fitted with a residual current-operated circuit breaker (RCB), which detects the slightest deviation in the current reaching the earth and automatically cuts off the power.

Choosing the lighting

Outdoor lights come in three main types. The first two are tungsten, which produces a warm, yellow light, and low-voltage tungsten halogen lights, which have a very white light that shows up the true colour of plants and accessories. Both of these are very economical to run once they have been linked to a suitable transformer. Third comes discharge lighting which is expensive to buy and uses sodium or mercury to produce a green-blue light which is good for highlighting dramatic foliage plants. You can have spotlights for highlighting plants and features; floodlights, which are useful for washing with light the back wall or a plant-smothered trellis; and downlighters for fixing into overhead features such as screens and pergolas. A combination of effects is best. You should also make sure any table or seating areas are well lit without creating an uncomfortable glare.

If certain lights can be operated individually then so much the better – flexibility means you can vary the effect according to your mood and the time of year. Candles, Chinese lanterns and bamboo flares with refillable oil reservoirs are also available for special party nights, or you could string a row of tiny electric fairy lights around a pergola or along overhead wires for a festive atmosphere.

CHAPTER FIVE

DECORATING AND FURNISHING

FURNITURE, PLANTS AND ACCESSORIES

You've made sure your balcony is safe and stable, it is suitably sheltered, screened from prying eyes, and all the major fittings have been planned and installed: if you have thought it all through carefully, a certain look and atmosphere will have started to develop. Now the really enjoyable aspect of owning and planning a balcony begins – that of choosing the decorations and furnishings that will reinforce the look and reflect your lifestyle.

Just like designing an interior room, there is great satisfaction and pleasure in finding exactly the right item or making a successful blend of co-ordinated colours or contrasting shapes. There will be plants to harmonize, furniture to add and accessories to find – all the flexible features that will add exactly the right finishing touches. It is worth taking time and trouble over your choice of these final elements; they contribute much to the overall look of the area and to your comfort and enjoyment in using it. These

A simple wooden bench completely enclosed by a dense screen of flowers and foliage makes a splendidly secluded area in which to sit and relax. In such private surroundings, the choice of plants will set the style and theme: maybe country cottage, or, as here, a dramatic blend of bold foliage plants and red flowers.

are also the items that can be changed or substituted from year to year, perhaps to create a totally different look or atmosphere, or simply to ring the changes.

SPECIAL EFFECTS

Before you start adding any furniture and furnishings, there may be a few special decorative effects you would like to consider that will bring just a little originality or a certain clever visual effect to your balcony scheme. An indoor/outdoor hybrid like this can take advantage of some of the more inventive *trompe-l'oeil* and design tricks usually reserved for the home, or sometimes the patio. Since the majority of effects are concerned with creating the impression of space within a rather limited area, they can be particularly appropriate once adapted and applied to an outdoor location such as a balcony.

Using colour successfully

Use of colour is one of your most effective tools: white and pale colours give the impression of light and space; darker colours draw it in and encourage a sense of drama and cosy seclusion. Plenty of white paint on trellis-work, plant containers and the back wall is a quick and easy way to add a cheery brightness, although beware of using too much of it on a hot sun-trap balcony as the glare will be unbearable. Pastel shades are softer but still give the impression of light and space: creams, pale blues, greens and greys, which are the smartest, most fashionable choice for modern balconies. These colours are widely available not just as paints for decorating walls and woodwork, but also as timber stains and varnishes should you wish to continue the theme over the floor decking or trellis, and in paving materials and fabrics for a completely co-ordinated look.

Trompe-l'oeil

People with more artistic talents and a sense of humour may like to try their hand at a *trompe-l'oeil* painting using a suitable range of exterior paints. This might take the form of a beautiful but fake view on a section of screening which in fact hides a much grimmer reality. On a dull concrete or

A carefully planned system of outdoor lighting, safely installed, extends the roof garden's use on summer evenings, and also provides a wonderfully illuminated vista through closed windows on winter nights.

brick back wall, you may prefer to paint a jungle of exotic plants or a trailing climber if you do not have the space or climate for the real thing. A vigorous vine permanently hung with luscious fruit would make a wonderful backdrop to a sophisticated outdoor dining area with, perhaps, a real, ornamental vine twining overhead to continue the joke. Tricks such as these look particularly effective when framed by an arch, a fake window, door or gateway encouraging the impression that the balcony extends further than it really does. The effect could be created using shaped sections of trellis, or slim stone or brick facings to match the existing wall. Painting these an all-over colour will successfully heighten the illusion.

Using mirrors

Another clever way to suggest that the balcony is in fact bigger than it actually is, or that there is something of great beauty just beyond its limits, is to insert a section of mirrored glass into an arch or alcove, effectively doubling the view of your balcony. This is especially stunning when it reflects a mass of well planned plants. If you really want to fool the onlooker that there is another lovely area through the arch, place light trellis-work over the mirrored glass as well, to confuse the eye still further.

PLANTS AND PLANTERS

Your most important accessories for colour co-ordinating, creating special effects and both softening and adding life to your balcony scheme, are the plants you choose. Previous chapters have already discussed plant collections for serving a particular purpose or generating a certain look.

If you are simply aiming at a good display amongst which to sit and relax or want to provide a year-round attractive view from the house, the guidelines are even simpler and the choice extensive. You might be surprised at the range of plants that will flourish in containers or small planters – even trees and shrubs can be good container subjects, providing they are kept adequately fed and watered. Some are obviously more suitable than others – the smaller, more compact and dwarf varieties, for example, or those that can be clipped or pruned to keep them in check. Standard-grown trees and shrubs – those which are trained to produce a neat ball of foliage (complete with flowers or fruit at the appropriate time of year) on top of a long narrow trunk – are particularly popular on balconies for their decorative value. However, the very fact that the roots of container-grown trees and shrubs are restricted will naturally limit their size.

Add to this list all the dramatic foliage plants, the bright summer flowers and fresh spring bulbs at your disposal, to be blended with the flowers and foliage of the climbing plants described in Chapter Four, and you will find that the design possibilities are endless for all seasons. Because all the plants have to be grown in pots and containers, the display is easy to maintain and keep in peak condition, as you simply replace plants once they are past their best or reorganize the containers. Another advantage is that the whole scheme is completely flexible: it can be reorganized or rejuvenated at a day's notice.

Creating a mature effect

Given the exciting scope and range of plant material, you may be feeling disappointed that the balcony area is so small and that your choice will have to be limited to only a few species each season. Be consoled by the fact that the area lends itself to cramming in a great many plants to create the stunning effect of a profusion of shape and colour. Unlike an ordinary garden, where young plants have to be given plenty

Cool but casual, this soft blue/grey scheme is highly fashionable and offsets a large expanse of brick. A skilfully painted trompe l'oeil vista adds a classical touch to an ultramodern setting.

of space to grow so the scheme does not really achieve the desired mature effect for a year or so, pots can be easily moved close together on a balcony and repositioned or replaced as needed.

For a good, balanced display, you should be aiming at not just year-round interest and harmonious or stunning colour combinations, but also an effective blend of different heights and shapes within your plant arrangements – remember with mixed groups that large plants should be positioned to the rear or centre, and smaller species to the front. Apart from showing them to their best advantage, this helps to build up a three-dimensional tiered effect: shelves or staging at different levels can also be used to create this rich impression of depth and maturity.

Using seasonal plants

To keep maintenance to a minimum, it makes sense to plan a permanent framework of small shrubby and evergreen plants to which you could add a changing display of more seasonal species, and which will also provide something of interest at those times of year when little else is in season. Glossy holly is reliable and a good container shrub; the yellow variegated types are particularly attractive and will add a splash of sunshine to the balcony on dull days. A dwarf rhododendron (in a pot of lime-free soil) makes a fine show of foliage all year round with the bonus of beautiful flowers in early summer. Alternatively, you could choose a hardy, shade-tolerant *Daphne* for its fragrant flowers, pretty *Choisya ternata* or, for contrast, the bold feathery foliage of a few ferns, which look particularly good grown in individual pots or tubs and can be added wherever you need a touch of fresh greenery.

Try to add to your collection a few good spreading evergreens to cover and soften the edges of containers; choose reliable and vigorous growers like trailing ivies or the Japanese spurge, *Pachysandra terminalis*. For interesting evergreen shapes and colours, dwarf conifers look very good in pots, either grown singly or, in larger planters, in miniature arrangements of different heights and shapes. They come in a vast range of shapes and sizes, from balls and pyramids to mounds and cones in all shades of blue, gold, grey and green. Another excellent all-seasons idea for balconies are pots of small clipped evergreen topiary shapes which might include spirals, cubes and cones as well as orbs and mounds; they are compact, attractive and can be positioned as easily and effectively as any accessory.

Bulbs and spring flowers

A well-planned selection of colourful bulbs and early flowering plants is a must for your containers in spring, providing an early taste of freshness and colour that can always be enjoyed through a door or window if the weather if not warm enough to venture outside. The smaller, more delicate blooms that appear at this time of year, maybe braving winter snows and frosts, are especially suited to growing in pots where they can be more easily appreciated: sweet scented grape hyacinth (*Muscari*), and tiny snowdrops (*Galanthus*) look delightful planted *en masse* in raised troughs, on shelves or in window boxes where they can be easily seen and smelt. Larger displays of narcissi and tulips (it is worth selecting the more ornamental types with unusual markings and double frilled forms) can make a real show and be an uplifting sight from indoors after the long gloomy days of winter.

The richly coloured flowers and lush foliage of primulas can also be relied on for a good display. Depending on the general style of your balcony or personal preference, you could choose the more exotic effect of an elegant Kaffir lily (*Clivia miniata*), delicate freesias or pretty foliaged *Erythronium*.

Growing annuals

Flowering shrubs and climbers will provide a certain amount of summer interest with their beautiful blooms, but as a general rule you will be looking to quick-growing annual plants for your main summer colour. There is such an extensive choice of shades, markings and forms that you can really enjoy yourself devising limited or multi-colour schemes as you would balance and co-ordinate soft furnishings in an interior design.

There are the traditional golden marigolds and sweet-smelling *Dianthus*, neon pink fuchsias and large-bloomed petunias, multi-flowered *Impatiens*, carpet-forming *Alyssum* and pretty blue or purple lobelias. That classic balcony flower, the pelargonium, comes in a great many forms, and is popular not only because both the flowers and foliage are so attractive but also because it will largely fend for itself in most climates.

You will want to include a variety of trailing and carpeting plants among your general selection, not just to soften the front edges of your containers or to hang from pots mounted on the wall and trellis, but also to cascade over the front of your balcony or transform hanging baskets into glowing orbs of colour and shape. The effect can be almost too rich, even crude, unless you balance these bright flowers with a few evergreens and plants known best for their interesting foliage. Guaranteed to add a variety of shape and texture are the evergreen glossy *Fatsia japonica*, fresh lime green euphorbias, ferns, hostas, grasses and bamboos.

Winter interest

There are even plants that will look good at the end of the season and possibly through the winter months too, adding a splash of colour and sometimes the bewitching sight and scent of winter flowers to your basic evergreen framework. Some, like cotoneaster, are valued for their bright winter berries, or you could lift your spirits by planting an evergreen with variegated foliage such as the gold/green Japanese honeysuckle, *Lonicera japonica* 'Aureo-reticulata'. Some varieties of heather and certain shrubs will even flower in winter; the winter jasmine, *Jasminum nudiflorum*, produces delicious scented flowers along its bare branches and is excellent for growing over trellises and pergola structures.

To brighten up your tubs and pots you can add colour with the beautifully delicate but shade-loving cyclamen; the orange cherry fruits of the winter cherry, *Solanum capsicastrum*, which makes a compact, bright green miniature bush and looks superb in troughs or boxes; or the tender but splendid Scarborough lily, *Vallota speciosa*, with its stunning red trumpet-shaped flowers. You will find further plant suggestions for all purposes and locations in Chapter Seven.

Choosing suitable containers

The right plant containers can be almost as important as the plants you grow in them. The wrong type and colour could totally ruin the effect you are trying to achieve – you only have to consider the striking effect of green foliage and bright scarlet flowers against a white tub, or the loss of

Show off a fine piece of sculpture by raising it on a wooden plinth, built to match well-stocked plant containers and a timber-decked floor.

An arrangement of unplanted pots and urns can be as stunning as any sculpture or ornament.

impact when red or orange is positioned against a backdrop of terracotta, to realize exactly how important your choice will be. For this reason, if you are aiming for maximum impact, you really ought to have some idea of what you are going to plant before you buy or design your containers. If you are also hoping to design an area with a distinct look or atmosphere, you will have to consider whether your containers reflect it: from the smartly formal slatted Versailles tubs to Mediterranean terracotta pots or well-weathered rustic barrels.

Size is also to be considered and plants may look equally effective as a special specimen in a single pot, or arranged in contrasting groups in larger planters, provided their size and scale are complementary. A small plant will look lonely and slightly ridiculous in an over-large container – it is much better to pot it on into a larger one as it grows – or a tall plant incongruous and unstable in a small pot.

Free-standing planters

There are a great many types of free-standing planter to choose from in addition to any built-in boxes, raised beds and containers you might have constructed in timber, and stained or painted to match other structural features. Pots and tubs look good grouped together, especially to round off a corner or fill up an empty-looking area. However, the best effect is achieved not by mixing different types of container within a single group or arrangement, but by aiming at a good combination of sizes and heights in one material or a selection of similar ones. To help spread the weight, plants in several smaller pots may be preferable to one large container; troughs and long narrow boxes are also useful as they will not concentrate all the weight of soil and plants on one spot.

When choosing containers, you should also bear in mind how weather resistant they are for your particular location and how much maintenance they will require. Glazed pots may not be frost-proof, for example, whereas unglazed terracotta pots are porous and will dry out quickly in hot weather so will need more frequent watering. Timber and metal containers usually require an annual rub-down and repainting or coating with non-toxic preservative.

Classic pots

There are stone urns and pots with a charming traditional appearance for an instantly mellow feel, although they can be rather too heavy for many balconies. Terracotta pots and troughs are equally traditional but have a more informal look even at their most decorative, and are perfect for clipped evergreens, herbs and Mediterranean sun-lovers. They may be as plain as the classic flower pot, available in a wide range of sizes up to one big enough for a small tree. Others might be decorated with a tooled design or applied relief decoration displaying classical figures or flowers. The prettiest (and most expensive) come in the shape of terracotta baskets complete with a weave design and twisted rope effect handle, or in quirky animal and bird shapes designed to hold mosses and small-leaved plants.

Wall-hanging plant containers are available in both stone and terracotta, often in the shape of a basket or classical head. Terracotta can be glazed or left plain, and pots are available with the necessary matching saucers which look very smart on the balcony. You can also buy glazed decorated pots with oriental patterns and designs on them which are especially attractive and particularly suited to an oriental or

decorative theme. They also generally have matching saucers to collect the excess water. Like stone, the larger ceramic and terracotta pots are heavy so you will have to watch their weight if you intend using lots of them.

Lightweight alternatives

Concrete containers are the modern alternative to terracotta, and need not be as heavy as you might expect, nor are they very expensive. The range of sizes is useful when you are looking for a large planter to take several plants, for concrete comes in a wide range of shapes, heights and sizes, from circular, square, rectangular or hexagonal designs, to low bowls or tall columns. The predominant and most usual colour is white, but there is no reason why you should not repaint them in any colour you choose to suit your particular balcony scheme.

Fibreglass is another modern material offering a wide range of practical yet decorative options. The big advantage of fibreglass for balconies is that it is the lightest of all the quality container materials and is available in a very large selection of designs, some of which convincingly imitate more traditional materials.

Timber is also worth considering for its relative lightness and versatility; from the inexpensive rustic wooden barrel or tub to the elegantly formal Versailles planter with its slatted sides and corner finials, usually available in a choice of natural stain or white-painted finish. Because they are large yet inexpensive, barrels are particularly suitable for growing larger, more permanent plants such as shrubs or trees, or groups of plants. They also retain moisture well so are easy to maintain. Before planting, you should make sure that the container has not been used to store anything toxic.

Unusual containers

Using second-hand receptacles like this can be useful for creating an instant mature and more mellow effect on the new balcony. Other useful plant containers might include old chimney pots, plastic-lined baskets, boxes and crates, which can be treated to a new coat of paint or varnish. Old stone or ceramic sinks are popular for raising on a plinth or shallow ledge and planting with a collection of alpines, heathers or other relatively low-growing plants.

Groups of matching containers ranged in different sizes such as these terracotta pots maximize the impact of your plants and can help to pull a theme together.

Plastic containers

The lightest and cheapest plant containers of all are plastic, and while they come in white or terracotta-coloured imitations of classic pot styles, they are never completely convincing and tend to look rather cheap and insubstantial. In fact, they do not last long because they are quick to crack or discolour, so apart from their weight advantage, they could be a false economy to buy. There are better quality, large plastic pots but their decorative use on the balcony is rather limited.

Maximizing wall space

Wall- and trellis-mounted containers are also of great importance in a balcony garden: not only are they good space-savers, but they add valuable interest at different heights. There are hanging baskets and metal hayracks to fix on to the back wall or a sturdy pergola, also window boxes and wall troughs to attach at the desired height for holding a selection of plants. If a strong trellis is not smothered in climbers, pots can be hung on or clipped directly to the framework, but don't forget that you will need some form of integral saucer or drip tray to prevent ruining the balcony floor. Remember, too, that these plants in particular will require regular watering as they are in the most exposed position of all and their soil will dry out quickly. They may need watering at least twice a day in very hot weather.

ORNAMENTS AND ACCESSORIES

As a stylish outdoor living area, a well-planned balcony has a place for a small selection of carefully chosen ornaments and accessories to add a touch of humour or originality to the total scheme. This might take the form of an individual piece of sculpture, displayed to full advantage in a corner against a background of greenery, or a smaller piece raised on a plinth where it will command immediate attention as a focal point, especially if carefully spotlighted at night.

A less expensive option is one of the many ornaments available from garden centres and the more tasteful specialist garden shops. You can buy classical statuary in a great many sizes and styles, from life-size figures and baskets of fruit to more whimsical stone pigs, terracotta geese or other creatures, to be positioned peeping out from around trellis, pots or tubs.

To reinforce an oriental atmosphere on the balcony, there are bowls, buddhas, little pagodas and stone lanterns to be added sparingly to your scheme. Some large pots and urns, especially the pretty glazed Chinese ginger jars, could be considered more as ornaments than plant containers. This is especially so when their necks are narrow in relation to their base, making them unsuitable for planting, or where urns have been made by a master potter to a unique design and finish, so are particularly attractive. They can look superb left empty and arranged in groups of different sizes, or incorporated into a collection of plant containers. With an eye for the unusual and interesting, even smooth sea-washed pebbles, a piece of driftwood, or an old metal birdcage can become a balcony ornament full of character and interest.

For any decorative piece, the right setting is essential for the best effect: surrounding the item with plants helps integrate it beautifully into the total scheme. Alternatively, you can highlight a piece of sculpture or ornament by giving it pride of place on a low platform, tall plinth or shelf.

Look out for small decorative features to add a finishing touch to your roof garden scheme: wall plaques, ornamental containers and whimsical stone and terracotta creatures.

Little bigger than a corridor, this cleverly decorated balcony finds the space and style to enjoy the great outdoors with an eye-catching red and white theme for both plants and furniture.

Sophisticated scheme of relaxed elegance carried through from antique painted backdrop with trompe l'oeil peacock on the cleverly disguised door, a subtle curtain of climbers and comfortable furniture that doubles for lounging or dining.

As private and pretty as any country garden, a mass of pink and mauve pelargoniums and a table set for tea places this tiny balcony corner in a sunny world of its own.

FURNITURE AND FURNISHINGS

Balcony furniture must be as practical as it is attractive; it needs choosing carefully, especially if you intend to store it under cover during the colder months, in which case it will be an advantage if it can be easily dismantled or folded away. Some owners of small, modest balconies are content with taking a few pieces of their existing lounging or dining furniture outside as and when required. This is all very well if you can be bothered, but there is no point if the upheaval involved frequently dissuades you from using the area. There is also the problem of damage and weathering – fabrics may fade and varnished timbers crack and peel in strong sunlight.

A better option for lounging and outdoor picnics might be a thick rug and a collection of large cushions, all of which can be easily stored. They could be kept indoors or in a dry, weatherproof storage box actually on the balcony. Many types of garden and patio furniture can actually be left outside all year round and are attractive enough for balcony use. The drawback is that most tend to be made from heavy-weight metal or timber: you may have to restrict your choice to the lighter plastic and aluminium frame furniture if you must keep weight to a minimum on your balcony.

Sitting comfortably

Comfort is an important consideration, too, as you will probably be spending a lot of time in your new outdoor living area once it is completed, either relaxing in a lounger or deckchair, or dining al fresco with family or friends. There are a great many types of seating to choose from, depending on whether you simply want somewhere to sit comfortably and read the paper or enjoy the view, or prefer the last word in luxury from which to soak up the sun. There are plain wooden benches, or more elegant traditional garden seats with ornamental backs. Matching chair and table sets can be elegant, traditional or rustic, and are available in every style, material and colour imaginable. Dining chairs might be up to the minute, non-fade plastic, or fully upholstered to match the sun umbrella and tableware that come with it in the same range. Simpler canvas chairs or wooden seats can also be surprisingly comfortable, with the advantage that they fold away when not in use.

For a strictly traditional balcony, you can buy Victorian-style cast metal chairs and tables imitating early wrought ironwork and which can be left outside all year round. Loungers are for the real sun lovers and might be made of light timber or bamboo for a rather colonial air, especially when surrounded by a lush jungle of green plants. You can use moulded plastic for the ultra modern look or heavily upholstered white plastic for a touch of Riviera or Hollywood pool-side luxury.

Temporary furnishings

Some balcony furniture may have to be brought into storage over the winter months, but the majority is designed to stay outside at least all summer. However, there are also temporary furnishings to consider adding to your scheme: soft furnishings and accessories that will only be brought out in fine weather but which are generally stored indoors. You might like to pin brightly coloured lengths of fabric to a trellis or a wooden framework, or to drape them over an overhead structure to provide shade in hot weather. There are also cushions to buy or make for extra comfort on hard seats, matching tablecloths and crockery for outdoor meals, candle holders, insect repellents, wine coolers plus all the other trappings of the well-furnished balcony.

CHAPTER SIX

CARE AND REPAIR

PLANT AND STRUCTURE MAINTENANCE

By its very nature, a balcony is relatively easy to maintain — hardly more trouble than a sitting room containing rather a lot of houseplants that need care and attention. This is not just because the area is usually small and compact; a tiled, paved or timber floor only needs a sweep and wash down to keep it looking good, while plants grown in containers mean no weeding, no mess and minimum maintenance. There are no lawns to mow, beds to dig or tall hedges to clip. Instead, there are just a few pruning and planting tasks, the annual responsibility of checking the main structure and keeping it in good repair, and a regular clean and tidy-up armed with a broom and a plastic refuse sack to prevent any build-up of dirt and disease, so the balcony and plants look in top condition at all times.

Maintenance equipment

One big advantage of having to tackle only minimum maintenance tasks is that you do not need a large collection of tools to keep the balcony looking good. This may be just as well as you will need somewhere close at hand to store them. If using a broom cupboard or some sort of storage in

A basic framework of evergreen plants keeps the balcony looking good all year round with minimum maintenance, while shorter-lived flowering species in smaller containers provide seasonal highlights. The main area should be kept free from dirt and debris by regular sweeping and an occasional wash-down.

the house is not practical, you will have to consider providing unobtrusive facilities on the balcony itself – the important thing is that they should be handy, otherwise regular jobs are too easily shirked. A built-in cupboard or bunker might fit conveniently into an unused corner or double as seating or staging.

For watering your plants, you will need a plastic watering can and possibly a hosepipe. Most importantly, you will have to decide from where you will fetch the water. A bibcock, or outdoor tap, on the balcony would save the mess and inconvenience of traipsing through the house. You will need a strong trowel and fork, secateurs and at least two sprayers – one to refresh and clean the plants with clear water, and the other marked and reserved for treating any infestation from pests and diseases. A broom and bucket will be among your most used tools, as they are essential for cleaning and collecting debris. A dustpan and brush would also be useful as there will be no flower beds to sweep dirt on to and you certainly should not sweep it off the edge of the balcony on to the heads of anyone passing below. Add to your list of essentials a pair of gardening gloves and possibly (although the majority of features are usually at a convenient height) a kneeling mat or stool for tending pots in comfort.

CARING FOR THE STRUCTURE

You should have put your balcony in a safe and good state of repair before you contemplated its design and furnishings. After that, an annual check-up should be sufficient to spot any major structural problems. Early spring or late autumn are probably the best times to call in an architect or structural engineer to assess the ravages of a scorching summer or storm-racked winter. Of course, if you spot any cracks, wear or other signs of damage or fatigue in the meantime, you should have them investigated immediately.

CARING FOR THE FIXTURES AND FEATURES

Because of their elevated position and exposure to wind, balconies tend to be prone to a great deal of dust and debris which, without regular cleaning, would soon make plants and features look grimy and untidy, especially when sited in towns and cities.

Everyday maintenance

Allowing the dirt to build up not only looks shabby but makes plants prone to wilting and disease. A quick sweep up is very little bother if tackled regularly, much as you clean your interior floors. It also helps to collect any dead material or debris whenever you see it, and put it into a large plastic sack for disposal. This could be kept tidily in an ornamental barrel, bin or built-in box, until it is full.

Much easier, though, would be to vacuum the area, which is not quite the crazy idea it sounds. There are various heavy-duty electric cleaners, sometimes called wet-and-dry vacuums, available these days, which are specially designed for use both in the home and on the patio or balcony. They will efficiently clean every type of surface including carpets, paving, tiles or timber. These powerful machines can cope with most types of garden debris from dead leaves and twigs to dirt and dust, and can even be adapted to suck up water or wash and clean hard surface flooring. Washing your balcony floor will not only keep it looking as good as new but also helps to lay the dust. A machine like this to replace your standard vacuum cleaner would be a real boon to a conscientious balcony owner.

A wet-and-dry heavy-duty vacuum can be used to rid the roof garden of dirt, debris and dead leaves, as well as cleaning floors indoors.

One job that need not be tackled quite so often, but whenever you think it necessary, is to give your containers a good wash down or even a scrub with a stiff brush to prevent a build-up of dirt and algae. Naturally, this does not apply to any surfaces where you might wish to encourage lichens and moss to grow and impart a weathered, mellow look, such as on terracotta pots.

Spraying plants regularly with clean water, especially during hot, dry weather, will also help to keep dust at bay and stop your plants looking tired and drab. Spraying has other benefits for your plants too: it will prevent leaves becoming clogged, buds dropping off and flowers withering and dying too quickly in hot weather. You should never spray foliage when the sun is at its hottest – early evening is the best time – as the heat may scorch and damage the leaves through the magnifying effect of the droplets. Spraying could be made a leisurely and pleasant task, giving you the opportunity to enjoy your plants at close quarters, and to look out for early signs of pests and diseases or pick off any dead material before problems can spread.

Cleaning the supports and floor

Structural materials are tough and keep themselves in reasonably good condition, provided they are cleaned occasionally. Once or twice a year, however, you should be prepared to give the balcony floor, and any supports not covered in climbing plants, a thorough inspection, checking for any signs of damage or wear and repairing accordingly.

Stains on concrete floors and pavers can be successfully cleaned off with a proprietary patio surface cleaner or diluted hydrochloric acid. Great care should be taken to wear

Liberal use of coloured paints and stains can co-ordinate fixtures, furniture and accessories or add new life to old or second-hand items. Here a smart grey has been extended to cover and disguise other immovable features such as drainpipes and built-in planters.

protective clothing and you should follow the manufacturer's instructions to the letter when handling dangerous chemicals, making sure they don't splash on to your plants or plant containers. Always wash down thoroughly with clean water afterwards, taking care that the waste water does not wash over the front of the balcony or drain away into any water butts you may have.

Timber decking needs scrubbing with a stiff brush to remove any slippery algae, after which softwoods should be treated with an appropriate preservative. The same treatment applies to any other timber features on the balcony such as built-in seating, plant containers and pergolas. Railings and other metal surfaces will need rubbing down and repainting only when they begin to show signs of weathering or peeling.

Looking after the furniture

Upholstered furniture is generally brought indoors during cold, wet weather. Plastic frames simply need a wipe-over, and fabrics can be replaced when they begin to wear, either as complete ready-made covers or made-to-measure from suitably fade-resistant material.

Timber seating can usually be left outside all year round. However, softwoods require annual repainting or varnishing – yacht varnish stands up to the sun and wind better than ordinary polyurethane, which tends to crack and blister. Hardwoods are more expensive but require minimal maintenance. Teak and iroko are usually cleaned with white spirit followed by a good scrub with soap and water, then an application of teak oil. Beech and elm should be rubbed down with fine sandpaper and treated with linseed oil.

Tubular steel and plastic-coated tables and dining chairs that are resistant to fading and cracking can also be left out on the balcony in all weathers, or stacked and folded if they are unlikely to be used over the winter. A wipe-down with a damp cloth and a spot of oil on any metal parts before the new spring season should be sufficient. This is also a good time to check and oil any awning mechanisms and other moving metal parts.

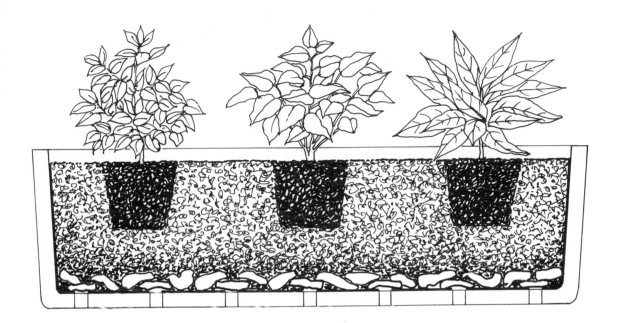

CARING FOR THE PLANTS

Being grown in pots and containers makes plants much easier to maintain, provided they have been properly planted and given the right kind of compost. Nevertheless, they do need careful watering and feeding if they are to flourish, as they can quickly dry out or the soil become impoverished. Pests and disease may also be a problem in the confined environment of a small balcony: the secret is to notice any infestation at the earliest opportunity and treat it before it spreads. Always try a mild remedy first, such as a soapy spray, and chemicals only as a last resort, handling them carefully.

CONTAINER PLANTING

Pots and tubs need good drainage. You can provide this either with drainage holes in the bottom of the container and a 2.5 cm (1 in) layer of crocks to prevent them getting clogged, plus a saucer, drip tray or trough to prevent any water damaging the balcony floor, or, where this is not practical, say in the case of window boxes, a layer of stones or crocks to a depth of about a third of the pot's size.

Add sufficient compost so that when the plant is inserted

Containers should incorporate a layer of crocks or pebbles for good drainage, topped with suitable compost. The plants must be positioned so that the top of the existing root ball is just below the rim of the container for non-spill watering.

there is room for about 1 cm (½ in) of new compost on top and a space of about 2.5 cm (1 in) for watering without it spilling over the sides of the container. Soil-less composts are lightest and should not be firmed down too hard, otherwise they become over-compacted. You should also take note of any plant's particular needs, such as an acidic or lime-based compost. After watering the plant in its original container, you should lift it carefully out of the pot, or slit its black plastic bag, and position it in the new container, adjusting the level as necessary and topping it up gently with new compost before watering it in.

Alpine plants

Because such stringent conditions are exacted on alpine plants in their native habitat, you will have to reproduce this environment as closely as possible, when growing all but the hardiest, most adaptable types. For this reason, alpines are usually grown in complementary collections of several species in a large container such as a trough or bowl. Around twenty different varieties can be grown in an old sink.

There are both acid- and lime-preferring types of alpines. All alpines prefer full sun and need to be sheltered from strong winds and early frosts, which may damage the delicate spring flowers. The soil does not need to be particularly fertile, although this produces plenty of foliage, but few flowers. However, it must be free draining with plenty of sharp grit and a good layer of gravel or pebbles in the bottom of the container. The soil should be kept completely weed-free; otherwise your plants can be quickly smothered. Never allow the soil to become water-logged or the shallow rooted plants will rot. On the other hand, it is equally important to keep the container well watered, especially in summer. Never allow the soil to dry out completely; mulching with a layer of stone chippings and the occasional boulder or rock for interest, will help slow down rapid evaporation from the soil's surface.

Planting up hanging baskets

Hanging baskets can be tricky to plant up, so prop them on a large flower pot or suspend them from a low hook while you are filling them. The wire or plastic-slatted basket should first be lined with sphagnum moss or a pre-formed synthetic liner.

A roof garden with an oriental or hi-tech theme embracing a permanent planting scheme and more sculptural features, tends to look good whatever the weather and time of year. Timber-decked fixtures only require an occasional scrub to remove dirt and algae and an annual treatment of an appropriate wood preservative.

A small saucer of stones in the bottom of the basket will help to preserve moisture as its exposed position makes it prone to drying out. The basket is generally filled with an appropriate compost and the plants inserted into the sides of the container to get all-round coverage of foliage and flowers.

Planting up floor-standing containers

For a mixed arrangement in a large floor-standing container, the tub, pot or trough should be filled with compost to within 2.5 cm (1 in) of the rim and the plants, in their original pots, arranged on top of the soil in their intended positions: tall plants to the centre, smaller species and trailers in the front. When you are happy with the arrangement, plant the larger ones first, digging appropriately sized holes with a trowel and firming the plants in. When all the plants are in place, water well and cover the surface with small stones or gravel to help retain moisture.

Underplanting for spring

When summer flowers have died back, you may like to underplant your winter greenery with spring bulbs. As a general rule, these are planted to a depth of around twice the diameter of the bulb. For a double display, plant the bulbs in two staggered layers, one on top of the other. Bulbs need good drainage, otherwise they will rot, so make sure the soil does not get too waterlogged; a little coarse grit mixed in when planting will help.

Planting up herb and strawberry pots

These are planted slightly differently from ordinary containers. With multi-pocketed herb and strawberry pots made from plastic or terracotta, you start with a good layer of drainage material such as broken crocks or small stones – about 7.5 cm (3 in) should be plenty. Begin to fill each pot with potting compost until you reach the level of the first hole, then insert the roots of one of your plants into the pocket and firm the soil around it. When all the holes on that level have been planted, carry on adding the compost until you reach the next level of holes, and so on. Each plant should be watered in as you proceed. When the container is fully planted, you can water from the top. Some forms of container have a central watering chute which is filled with drainage material.

Planting up potato barrels

For a compact crop of potatoes, the technique is slightly different again. You must put a drainage layer of crocks, about 15 cm (6 in) deep, in a wooden barrel or plastic bin and then an equal layer of compost – a rich well-fertilized mixture with plenty of sand to aid drainage is best. Place four or five seed potatoes on top of the compost, then cover them with another 15 cm (6 in) layer of compost and water lightly. When these potatoes have shooted and are showing about 15 cm (6 in) above the surface, add more compost so that just the tips are showing. Keep earthing up in this way until you reach the top of the barrel. You can plunge your arm into the tub and test the size of the potatoes before you dig them up.

Enjoy the pleasure of potatoes with a roof garden barrel.

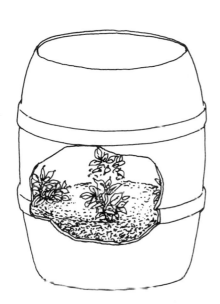
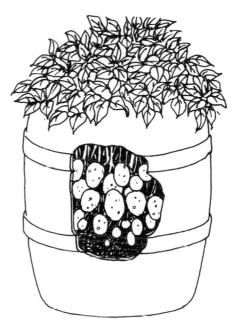

WATERING THE PLANTS

Watering is the most tedious chore in the balcony garden, although there are clever ways of reducing even this task to a minimum. The large number of plants in containers means a heavy watering commitment, especially if the weather is hot and dry. Both sun and wind can be terribly drying; water also evaporates out of the top of the pot, and in the case of porous material like terracotta, out of the sides of the container too.

Neglecting to water causes real problems, for once the compost has become completely dried out it can be difficult to moisten it properly again. Plants will soon suffer and may even die. Positioning the containers close together helps to create a mini climate and preserve moisture. There is also the advantage that you do not have to travel far between plants on your watering sessions, unlike in a garden.

Surface mulching helps to reduce moisture loss from the surface; peat or chopped bark tends to blow away on the balcony, so it is better to use gravel, granite chips or small pebbles, which have the advantage of looking attractive too. When watering, check that the water filters through the compost properly before it starts to fill the drip tray or saucer. If it rushes through at speed, the compost is too dry and you must prick it with a small garden fork or a skewer to allow more air in and let the water penetrate it properly. The best time to water is after the sun has gone down, or at least lost its strength, so the water does not immediately evaporate in the heat. This also gives the plant plenty of time to absorb sufficient moisture. There are automatic watering systems available which may be useful if you lead a very busy life or have to go away. You can also buy self-watering containers which incorporate an integral reservoir that needs topping up only occasionally.

FEEDING THE PLANTS

Plants grown in containers also quickly exhaust their supply of nutrients and must be regularly fed, especially during the spring and summer months, if they are to grow and flourish. This is particularly important for herbs, fruits and vegetables subjected to regular picking.

Fertilizers recommended for different types of plants are available in a wide range of easy-to-apply formats. You can use pills, pellets and sticks which are inserted in the soil, or quicker-acting (and thus more effective but more time-consuming) foliar feeds which are made up and sprayed on to the plants' foliage. Liquid feeds should be applied about once a week during the growing season, and the soil-applied granular fertilizers approximately once a month. Always follow the manufacturer's instructions on making up and applying the fertilizer, as overfeeding or using too strong a mixture can be more damaging to your plant than completely starving it of food. It is up to you whether you use an organic or chemical fertilizer.

Permanent roof garden plants require very little attention, except perhaps an annual prune for flowering climbers like these roses to encourage plenty of blooms next year.

Supports for climbing plants: a system of horizontal wires for a twining shrub such as clematis; honeysuckle trained up a stout section of trellis; and self-clinging ivy or Virginia creeper smothering a wall.

GENERAL PLANT MAINTENANCE

Balcony plants need little maintenance; flowering species should be dead-headed, and any dead leaves and broken or distorted stems removed as and when you see them. This encourages fresh blooms and helps to keep the plants looking good and free of disease. A bucket or plastic sack is a good way of disposing of the debris cleanly and efficiently. At the end of the year, give the whole area a general tidy-up and keep dead leaves under control by sweeping or vacuuming them up regularly. Snow should be gently knocked off over-wintering plants to avoid its weight bending or snapping their branches.

The beauty of a completely contained garden is that you can replace any plant which is past its best with a new pot or plant to maintain your display in peak condition at all times. This also helps you to produce something of interest right through the seasons. Try to be ruthless and don't be tempted to let a short-lived plant completely die off before replacing it; it will only add a jarring note to your arrangement and it is possible that the plant could introduce disease to the soil as it decays.

Repotting plants

More permanent plants will eventually outgrow their containers and need potting on to larger pots or tubs of fresh compost. The best time for potting on and repotting is before the new growing season starts and while the plant is resting. Some plants like to have their roots restricted but you can tell if a plant is pot-bound because it will lose condition or stop growing. To check if this is so, tap the container gently to loosen the plant and examine the rootball to see if it is a matted mass of roots, which may even have started to grow out of the drainage holes. The new container should allow about 4 cm (1½ in) of extra space for new root growth – too large a pot will inhibit growth just as effectively as one that is too small. Replant carefully as described earlier in this chapter.

Eventually, perennial plants will reach the size you require, or you may not have room for a larger container. If this is the case, plants can be repotted in the same size container after you have first reduced the size of the rootball to limit its growth. This is done by gently removing the

Vegetables such as peppers and tomatoes can be successfully grown and ripened on a sheltered roof garden provided that the heavy trusses of fruit are given some kind of support such as this system of canes.

plant from its pot and trimming away about 5 cm (2 in) of the rootball with a pair of sharp scissors, cutting out any dead roots. Repot in fresh compost exactly as you would a new plant.

Staking plants

Tall plants may require staking to prevent wind damage. Split canes or lengths of slender bamboo can be pushed into the soil in containers and tied with green twine (for soft-stemmed plants) or covered metal ties (for woody stems). There are also special metal supports you can buy which are inserted in the compost while the plant is still small so that it can grow up through them.

TRAINING AND PRUNING PLANTS

Because you often want plants to be decorative or trained to fit a particular size or shape, training and pruning plays an important part in the balcony garden. Pinching out the tops of plants will encourage good bushy growth and prevent them getting leggy. Some plants, such as heather and shrubby herbs, can be lightly clipped after flowering to keep their desired shape. Only shrubs, trees and climbers will require any kind of formal pruning and even that should be just enough to maintain a good shape or to encourage flowering. Hard pruning produces vigorous growth, while a lighter pruning encourages more flowers and fruit.

Pruning shrubs

Flowering shrubs should be cut back in spring or late summer after they have bloomed. This is a good opportunity to get rid of any dead or diseased material and will encourage strong shoots next season. Cutting back the stems of a pot-grown rose by about half after the first frost will prevent wind damage in winter.

Climbing plants and shrubs will require appropriate support: some like ivy are self-clinging, using aerial roots or sucker tips to attach themselves to any vertical surface. Others, including many climbing shrubs, have curling tendrils or twining stems that can be trained up trellis, or along galvanized wires. Many heavy or bushy shrubs will need tying in to provide extra support.

Pruning climbers

Light climbers like ivies need only trimming into shape. Vigorous flowering climbers, such as jasmine and honeysuckle, do not normally require pruning unless you want to reduce a tangled mass, but it is a good idea to remove any dead or diseased stems to keep the plant in good health. Evergreen climbers are generally pruned in early spring and deciduous types in winter. Wisteria is normally pruned in mid-summer, cutting the side shoots back to about 15 cm (6 in), and again in mid-winter when they are shortened to two buds. Cut back the side shoots of climbing roses to within one or three buds of the main stem; rambling roses can be completely cut back after flowering. Clematis plants are pruned according to their group, so check that with your supplier before proceeding.

Pruning soft fruit bushes

If you want to try growing fruit on a small balcony, perhaps against a sunny wall or trellis, then pruning a soft fruit bush

114

into a pot-grown bush, or growing one of the two-dimensional trained effects, is probably the only way you will find the space. With soft fruit, the new side shoots are pruned back to the main stem until the desired shape is reached. Many trees and soft fruits can be grown in fan shapes to enable the branches to receive the maximum amount of sunshine. There are also cordon and espalier forms, involving strict pruning and tying techniques, to create horizontal forms that encourage maximum fruiting in the minimum of space. A specialist book will advise on the best way to prune and train fruiting trees and shrubs.

Pruning to achieve an ornamental effect

Other ornamental features are possible if you have the patience; fast-growing evergreen trailers and climbers can be trained over wire shapes to produce a quick topiary effect. Alternatively, slow-growing, small-leaved evergreens, such as privet, yew and box, can be clipped into formal shapes if you have the patience. Clipping normally takes place at the end of summer.

Standards are also popular for balcony containers and many shrubby or semi-shrubby plants, such as roses, fuchsias, fruit trees and bay trees, can be trained into this classic tall-stemmed lollipop form. This involves removing all the side shoots from the main stem of a rooted cutting but leaving the foliage on top. When the plant reaches the required height, the top is removed and the side shoots are allowed to develop, with the growing tips pinched out to encourage bushy growth until the required shape is achieved.

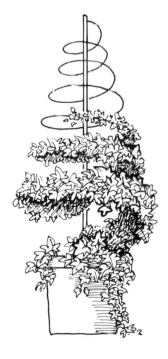

Climbing plants such as ivy and evergreen honeysuckle can be trained over wire shapes to create a topiary effect quickly and easily.

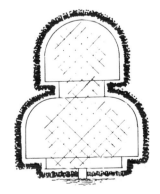

CHAPTER SEVEN
PLANT LISTS

Heights given are a guide to scale only as container-grown plants will be naturally limited in their growth.
('T' denotes a tender species suited to tropical or sub-tropical climates.)

ORNAMENTAL TREES AND SHRUBS

Plant	Approx Height	Character
Abelia × grandiflora	90 cm (35 in)	Small semi-evergreen shrub with tiny pink or white flowers in summer.
Acacia (T)	1–3 m (3–10 ft)	Assorted varieties offer attractive foliage and usually golden flowers.
Acer palmatum (Japanese maple)	2 m (6½ ft)	Attractively shaped foliage, and spring and autumn interest. Some hybrids are more like small shrubs and are ideal for growing in containers. A. p. 'Atro-purpureum', for example, has purple coloured foliage; the 'Dissectum' form is distinguished by its delicate feathery foliage.
Arundinaria japonica (Pseudosasa japonica)	4–5 m (13–16 ft)	A hardy bamboo that thrives in half shade and which has glossy dark green ribbon-like leaves on slender canes. Compost must be kept moist.
Arundinaria murieliae (Fargesia spathacea) (Elegant bamboo)	2.4–3 m (8–10 ft)	An attractive bamboo with bright green canes which turn yellow-green.
Berberis	30–230 cm (12–90 in)	Both evergreen and deciduous forms of this easily grown and attractive prickly shrub have fine spring flowers and showy fruits. B. 'Nana' is slow growing and mound forming; B. × antoniana is an evergreen, also rounded, with deep yellow flowers and blue-black berries.
Buxus sempervirens (Box)	30–40 cm (12–16 in)	Classic slow-growing evergreen with tiny, glossy green leaves for clipping into hedge and topiary shapes. Some forms are ornamental in themselves: B. s. 'Elegantissima' makes a natural dome shape and has white markings; 'Gold Tip' has yellow tips.
Camellia japonica 'Adolphe Audusson'	2.4 m (8 ft)	A compact evergreen camellia with large blood-red flowers. Tolerates part shade.

Caryopteris	1 m (3 ft)	Small shrub valued for the soft effect of its grey leaves and blue flower spikes.
Chamaecyparis lawsoniana (Lawson cypress)	2 m (6½ ft)	Popular cypress with drooping green foliage.
Chamaerops humilis (Fan palm) (T)	6 m (20 ft)	This spiky palm is a slow grower so is usually much smaller than the maximum height specified.
Choisya ternata (Mexican orange)	3 m (10 ft)	Prized for its fragrant white flowers in late spring and early summer and its glossy dark green leaves which are also aromatic when bruised. The smaller evergreen C. t. 'Sundance' has light yellow young foliage.
Cordyline australis (Cabbage palm)	4.6 m (15 ft)	Sword-like evergreen leaves and small creamy summer flowers.
Corylus avellana 'Contorta' (Cork-screw hazel)	4.6–7.5 m (15–25 ft)	Small hazel grown for its ornamental spiral stems and showy catkins in late winter often shrubby.
Cotoneaster		Choose from a large number of types, most of which have ornamental berries useful for late summer interest. *C. apiculatus* makes arching stems of small round leaves and red fruits, yet does not grow too large. Prostrate forms grow to 30 cm (12 in); others may reach 5.5 m (18 ft).
Crataegus (Thorn)	4.6 m (15 ft)	Small ornamental trees with decorative fruits and fine spring blossom. *C. oxyacantha* 'Paul's Scarlet' has red double flowers.

Some fruit trees can be trained into an espalier or fan format in which the horizontal branches take up very little space against a wall or trellis.

Cycas media (T)	6 m (20 ft)	Australian palm-like cycad with deep green pointed fronds. Drought resistant.
Daphne	1.2 m (4 ft)	Choose the smaller hybrids of this shrub, valued for its scented flowers in late winter/early spring; make sure the container is well drained. *D. laureola* is a shade-loving evergreen with yellow green flowers. *D. mezereum* thrives in light shade and has purple red flowers and red berries; *D. m.* 'Alba' has white flowers and amber fruits; 'Rosea' has rose pink flowers. *D. odora* forms offer a similar range of colours and are shade-tolerant evergreens.
Euonymus fortunei	45 cm (18 in)	Various forms with attractive foliage for winter interest. Choose the smaller types such as 'Emerald and Gold' which is bushy with gold markings, turning pink in winter; or 'Silver Queen' which has white markings.
Fatsia japonica (False castor oil plant)	2 m (6½ ft)	A dramatic evergreen with glossy, palmate foliage which prefers part shade.
Festuca (Fescue grass)	23 cm (9 in)	Good foliage contrast plant with its evergreen blue/grey mound of spiky stems.
Gardenia jasminoides (T)	2 m (6½ ft)	Evergreen with strong-scented white flowers.
Hydrangea macrophylla (Lacecap hydrangea)	1.5 m (5 ft)	The large blooms come in various colours: for example, 'Geoffrey Chadbuned' which is red, 'Blaumeise' which is blue and 'White Wave' which is white.
Ilex (Holly)	120 cm (48 in)	Many forms and colours, with or without spines. Variegated types are useful for different effects. Markings may be yellow, gold, white, cream or silver; stems could be purple, black or green and berries black, red, round or oval. Plants are unisexual so a male plant and a female one must be grown if berries are to be produced. However, many people find the foliage attractive enough in itself – especially in the case of ornamental hollies and pot-planted clipped hollies that are not allowed to berry in any case.
Juniperus (Juniper)	10–250 cm (4–98 in)	A wide choice of varieties whose coloured, needle-like foliage is useful in winter. *J. chinensis* 'Pyramidalis' makes a slow-growing conical blue bush; spreading 'Gold Coast' is golden yellow; 'Embley Park' has drooping branches of grass green leaves.

One of the very best dwarf maples for growing in tubs or pots: the tiny Acer palmatum *'Dissectum Atropurpureum' with its delicately divided and unusually coloured foliage.*

Many small trees or shrubs will flourish on the roof garden in a tub or large pot: if you wish to grow tender species such as a citrus fruit, bay tree or subtropical shrub, this enables you to bring the plant under cover during the colder months.

Laurus nobilis (Sweet bay)	1.5 m (5 ft)	Classic evergreen shrub or standard grown tree for sheltered areas. Glossy green laurel-shaped leaves are aromatic and can be used in cooking. Foliage often clipped into decorative shapes.
Lavandula (Lavender)	45–100 cm (18–40 in)	Highly aromatic and sun-loving small shrub which has various forms, all of which are evergreen. *L. angustifolia* 'Alba' has white flowers and narrow grey-green foliage; *L. a.* 'Rosea' has soft pink flowers and a compact habit; 'Munstead' is larger but also compact with lavender blue flowers.
Malus (Flowering crab)	3.6 m (12 ft)	Small ornamental trees valued for their stunning spring blossom and interesting autumn fruits. there are many small varieties such as 'Golden Hornet' which has white flowers and plenty of yellow fruits; 'John Downie' whose large orange-red fruits are edible; and 'Red Jade' or 'Royal Beauty' which has red fruits and a weeping habit.
Miscanthus sacchariflorus	2.4 m (8 ft)	Spectacular hardy grass which makes a dense clump of long, flat, dark green ribbons. *M. sinensis* 'Zebrinus' has handsome gold stripes.
Musa ornata (T)	150 cm (60 in)	Small flowering banana with red and yellow flowers and small fruits.
Nandina domestica (Heavenly bamboo)	2.4 m (8 ft)	A pretty bamboo with delicate pinnate leaves, white flowers and red berries.
Phalaris arundinacea var. *picta* (Ribbon grass)	60–100 cm (24–40 in)	Attractive green and white grass also known as 'gardeners' garters'.

Phormium tenax	2.4 m (8 ft)	A good architectural foliage plant with large sword-like leaves. Hybrids offer colour options: bronze ('Bronze Baby'); black ('Dark Delight'); red markings ('Maori Chief'); apricot ('Apricot Queen'), even cream, purple and pink variations.
Phyllostachys aurea (Golden bamboo)	2.4–3 m (8–10 ft)	Evergreen bamboo with green canes that turn yellow.
Prunus (Flowering cherry)	6 m (20 ft)	Useful small trees producing excellent blossom and foliage colours. *P. rufa* 'Himalayan Cherry' has the added attraction of peeling red-brown or amber bark; *P. subhirtella* 'Autumnalis', the autumn cherry, and its double or weeping hybrids flower at the end of summer.
Pyrus (Ornamental pear)	4.5 m (15 ft)	A group of small trees useful for special effects. For example, *P. salicifolia* 'Pendula', the weeping silver pear, which has a weeping habit and silver foliage; *P. communis* 'Beech Hill' has good autumn colour.
Rhapis humilis (T)	150 cm (60 in)	Low-growing palm excellent for pots.
Robinia pseudoacacia 'Frisia' (False acacia)	5.4 m (18 ft)	A small tree with attractive golden yellow foliage from spring to autumn.
Rosmarinus (Rosemary)	30–120 cm (12–48 in)	Shrubby herb which enjoys full sun and looks good in tubs. Needle-like foliage is grey-green and the tiny flowers are blue.
Salix (Willow)	3 m (10 ft)	Wide choice of shrub or tree forms, many with attractive foliage and interesting catkins, such as *S. helvetica* or *S. lanata*, the woolly willow, which is a downy slow grower.
Sorbus (Rowan)	5.4 m (18 ft)	Attractive foliage providing interest in spring, summer and autumn. Many have good berries too: 'Joseph Rock' (gold); 'Pearly King' (white/pink); *S. scalaris* (red berries).
Taxus baccata (Yew)	2.4 m (8 ft)	Sombre dark green evergreen conifer which lends itself to being clipped into hedge and topiary shapes. It is a slow grower, so could be grown in a container.
Thryptomene (T)	1 m (3 ft)	Tiny leaves and small pink flowers throughout the year.
Trachycarpus fortunei (Hardy palm)	2–3 m (6½–10 ft)	A good architectural foliage plant with dramatic fan-shaped leaves.
Viburnum davidii	75 cm (30 in)	Smallest of the viburnums, with glossy leaves and light blue berries.
Yucca	1–2 m (3–6½ ft)	Dramatic foliage plant with sword-shaped leaves and creamy-white flower spikes.

HARDY FERNS

Adiantum pedatum (Maidenhair fern)	25 cm (10 in)	Frost hardy acid-loving fern with dainty foliage.
Asplenium trichomanes (Spleenwort)	7.5–15 cm (3–6 in)	Produces thread-like black stalks with green lobes.
Athyrium filix-femina (Lady fern)	30 cm (24 in)	Makes tufts of light green fronds.
Blechnum penna-marina	7.5–10 cm (3–4 in)	Young fronds have a coppery colour. This low-growing fern makes a carpet of small flattened fronds with more erect short fertile fronds.
Blechnum spicant (Hard fern)	25–30 cm (10–12 in)	Useful fern because it tolerates dry conditions.
Dryopteris dilatata (Broad buckler fern)	60–100 cm (24–40 in)	Has broad, divided fronds.
Dryopteris filix-mas (Male fern)	60–100 cm (24–40 in)	Reliable fern frequently seen in the wild. Produces a large clump of tough green fronds.
Matteuccia struthiopteris (Ostrich feather fern)	1–1.5m (3–5 ft)	Attractive ornamental fern with large feathery fronds.
Onoclea sensibilis (Sensitive fern)	50 cm (20 in)	Pretty fern that prefers moist conditions.
Osmunda regalis (Royal fern)	1.2–2 m (4–6½ ft)	Large dramatic clump of fronds.
Phyllitis scolopendrium (Hart's tongue fern)	50 cm (20 in)	A good contrast with flat tongue-like fronds covered in brown spores. An evergreen useful for winter interest.
Polypodium vulgare (Common polpody)	25–30 cm (10–12 in)	Good evergreen that tolerates chalk.
Polystichum aculeatum (Hard shield fern)	50–60 cm (20–24 in)	An evergreen with strong, dark green fronds.
Polystichum lonchitis (Holly fern)	30–100 cm (12–40 in)	Makes dense tufts of evergreen fronds.
Polystichum setiferum 'Plumosodivisilobum' (Soft shield fern)	50 cm (20 in)	Finely divided feathery fronds.

Long-flowering and easy to grow marigolds adding a splash of summer brilliance to a more permanent arrangement of holly, juniper and colourful Japanese maple.

HOSTAS

Hosta albomarginata	15–20 cm (6–8 in)	Narrow light green leaves with cream margins. Striped flowers are mauve and white.
H. fortunei 'Albopicta'	40–50 cm (16–20 in)	Oval yellow-edged leaves which develop dark green margins with age. There is a completely yellow form for spring and summer colour, 'Aurea'.
H. 'Frances Williams'	50–60 cm (20–24 in)	Spectacular blue-grey leaves with beige markings.
H. 'Halcyon'	30 cm (12 in)	Heart-shaped blue leaves and lilac flowers on purple stems.
H. 'Honeybells'	30 cm (12 in)	Mauve flowers are scented. Leaves are green.
H. lancifolia	15–18 cm (6–7 in)	Narrow shiny green leaves.
H. sieboldiana 'Elegans'	60 cm (24 in)	Large, round silver-grey leaves with deep indentations.
H. 'Thomas Hogg'	30 cm (12 in)	Deep green leaves have a wide cream margin. Summer flowers are lilac.
H. undulata	50 cm (20 in)	Wavy green leaves have a central white band.

ALPINES

Alyssum	Cushion-forming mass of tiny flowers can be white, yellow or pink.
Armeria	Makes a green mat below a mass of pink pompom heads.
Aubrietia	Popular mat-forming alpine with dense display of mauve, purple or red flowers.
Campanula (Bellflower)	Tussocks of pretty blue to mauve bell- or star-shaped flowers.
Chrysanthemum hosmariense (Alpine chrysanthemum)	Silver leaves and daisy-like flowers from spring to autumn.
Cyananthus (Trailing bellflower)	Mat-forming trailer with coloured foliage and blue flowers.
Cypripedium	Stunning group of orchids, some of which are very hardy.

Dianthus (Rock pinks)	A wide range of sweet-scented pink to almost red flowers with stripes and other markings.
Edelweiss	Woolly foliage and small white felt-like flowers.
Gentiana (Gentian)	Slender narrow leaves and beautiful blue trumpet flowers.
Helianthemum (Rock rose)	Like a tiny wild rose.
Potentilla (Cinquefoil)	Colourful summer plant with frondy foliage and rose-like blooms.
Primula	Familiar favourites for spring with their clumps of thick-veined leaves and beautiful deep-coloured blooms.
Ramonda	Rosette-forming plant with rough hairy leaves and mauve blue flowers.
Saxifrage	A large group of plants with interesting clump-forming foliage and pretty flower clusters.
Sedum (Stonecrop)	A wide range of sprawling plants with small fleshy evergreen leaves and heads of pink or yellow flowers.

Geraniums are guaranteed to make a spectacular and continuous summer display of bright colour for very little care and attention in most balcony locations.

HEATHS AND HEATHERS

Calluna vulgaris	10–60 cm (4–24 in)	There are many interesting hybrid forms of the evergreen common heather or ling. These are just a few of the colour variations.
C. *v.* 'Alba Plena'	50 cm (20 in)	Double white flowers in summer.
C. *v.* 'Beoley Gold'	45 cm (18 in)	Late summer white flowers and golden leaves.
C. *v.* 'Blazeaway'	50 cm (20 in)	Mauve flowers in late summer; leaves turn red in winter.
C. *v.* 'Gold Haze'	50 cm (20 in)	White flowers and gold foliage.
C. *v.* 'Orange Queen'	60 cm (24 in)	Pink flowers and gold foliage which turns orange.
C. *v.* 'Robert Chapman'	30–60 cm (12–24 in)	Mauve flowers and golden leaves which turn orange and then red.
C. *v.* 'Silver Queen'	60 cm (24 in)	Silver-grey leaves and pale mauve flowers.
C. *v.* 'Sister Anne'	10 cm (4 in)	Grey foliage with pink flowers.
C. *v.* 'Tib'	30–60 cm (12–24 in)	Double rosy-red flowers.
Erica arborea (Tree heath)	25 cm (10 in)	Fragrant white flowers in early spring. Hybrids produce purple flowers.
E. carnea (Winter heath)	25 cm (10 in)	Winter-flowering, lime-tolerant heather offering a wide choice of colours such as: 'Adrienne Duncan', with red flowers and dark bronze green foliage; 'Foxhollow', which has pale pink flowers and yellow foliage with a red tinge in winter; 'Pink Spangles' makes a mass of pink flowers in winter; 'Springwood White' has white winter blooms.
E. cinerea (Bell heather)	15–25 cm (6–10 in)	Summer-flowering in a wide choice of colours.
E. mediterranea	2 m (6½ ft)	Very tall, with rose-red spring flowers. Lime tolerant. Hybrids include grey and green foliage and white flowers.
E. vagans (Cornish heath)	1.2 m (4 ft)	Makes long sprays of flowers from summer through to autumn. There are many varieties with pink, white and cerise flowers and yellow foliage.

CONIFERS

Abies concolor 'Compacta'	60–90 cm (24–35 in)	A dwarf fir with an irregular rounded habit and bright silver-blue leaves.
A. koreana	1.5–2 m (5–6½ ft)	Dark green upper leaves are silvery-white beneath with attractive blue cylindrical cones.
A. nordmanniana 'Golden Spreader'	20–30 cm (8–12 in)	A neat bush of golden yellow needles.
Cedrus libani 'Sargentii'	60–90 cm (24–35 in)	Weeping habit produces a dense spread of green.
Chamaecyparis lawsoniana 'Aurea Densa'	30–50 cm (12–20 in)	Makes a dense dome of golden yellow foliage.
C. l. 'Ellwood's Pillar'	75–100 cm (30–40 in)	Produces a narrow compact pillar of feathery blue-grey.
C. l. 'Gnome'	20–30 cm (8–12 in)	A tiny deep green specimen.
C. l. 'Little Spire'	1.5–2 m (5–6½ ft)	Grows slowly into a green column which eventually produces attractive red 'flowers' in spring.
C. l. 'Nana Albospica'	75 cm (30 in)	White foliage looks almost like snow in summer.
C. l. 'Pygmy'	30 cm (12 in)	Makes a tiny mound of grey-green leaves.
C. pisifera 'Gold Spangle'	90 cm (35 in)	Rounded habit and bright gold foliage for good winter colour.
C. p. 'Plumosa Compressa'	20–30 cm (8–12 in)	Makes a tiny, compact mound of pale yellow foliage.
C. p. 'Plumosa Purple Dome'	50–60 cm (20–24 in)	Feathery grey foliage has a purple tint in winter.
C. thyoides 'Rubicon'	60 cm (24 in)	Compact bronze-green foliage turns a rich red in winter.
Cryptomeria japonica 'Compressa'	30–40 cm (12–16 in)	Small and compact forming a flat-topped globe of green foliage tinted a reddish-purple in winter.
C. j. 'Vilmoriniana'	30–40 cm (12–16 in)	Grows slowly to produce a neat globe of fresh green.
Microbiota decussata	20–30 cm (8–12 in)	Low-growing spread of lacy but dense green foliage which turns bronze in winter.
Picea abies 'Little Gem'	20–30 cm (8–12 in)	Makes a dense ball of green with attractive new shoots in spring.
P. glauca 'Aurina'	40 cm (16 in)	This fresh green, compact pyramid is the ideal miniature for sink and container gardens.

P. mariana 'Nana'	15–20 cm (6–8 in)	Slow-growing blue ball perfect for troughs and sinks.
Pinus mugo 'Humpy'	30–40 cm (12–16 in)	Makes a dense round bush of short green needles and prominent winter buds.
P. m. 'Wintergold'	40–50 cm (16–20 in)	Bright golden form through winter turning light green during summer.
P. pumila 'Dwarf Blue'	40–50 cm (16–20 in)	Slow-growing spreader producing clusters of blue and white needles.
P. strobus 'Reinshaus'	60 cm (24 in)	Small compact bush needs good drainage. Makes a dense display of glaucous needles.
P. sylvestris 'Hibernica'	50–60 cm (20–24 in)	Makes a compact round bush of grey-blue needles and prominent winter buds.
Taxus baccata 'Corley's Coppertip'	30–40 cm (12–16 in)	Copper-coloured leaves turn to green with whitish markings. Semi-prostrate form.
T. b. 'Summergold'	40–50 cm (16–20 in)	Bright golden yellow foliage in summer.
Thuja occidentalis 'Danica'	30–45 cm (12–18 in)	Compact globe of dark green turns bronze in winter.
T. orientalis 'Golden Ball'	40–50 cm (16–20 in)	Dome-shaped bush of bright yellow turns green and later bronze.
T. plicata 'Rogersii'	30–45 cm (12–18 in)	Good for winter colour, turning from green to golden bronze.
Tsuga canadensis 'Jeddeloh'	30–40 cm (12–16 in)	Graceful light green foliage and semi-prostrate habit.

PLANTS FOR SPRING INTEREST

Cheiranthus cheiri (Wallflower)	38–45 cm (15–18 in)	Useful rich early colour – plant in tubs when bushy before winter. Look out for the new compact forms in pastel colours.
Chionodoxa (Glory of the snow)	7.5–10 cm (3–4 in)	Grown for its pretty blue star-shaped flowers.
Clivia miniata (Kaffir lily)	50 cm (20 in)	Very elegant with bold, tongue-like leaves and large clusters of orange, trumpet-shaped blooms.
Crocus	5–13 cm (2–5 in)	Plant in massed groups to get the best effect from their low carpet of bright, waxy colour. They are good for planting under taller spring flowers and offer a choice of large or small, open or closed blooms, and a range of colours from purples, golds, pinks and whites to striped patterns.
Cyclamineus narcissi	20–30 cm (8–12 in)	Various colour types and a dwarf habit that makes them excellent for tubs.
Erythronium	30 cm (12 in)	There are various types with their lovely spotted foliage and beautiful nodding blooms, useful since they will tolerate light shade. The trout lily, *E. californicum*, has cream flowers; *E. dens-canis*, dog's tooth violet, has mauve to pink flowers.
Freesia refracta	50 cm (20 in)	Sweet-scented, delicate flowers in a blend of clear, complementary colours.
Galanthus (Snowdrop)	10–25 cm (4–10 in)	These tiny heralds of spring are usually the first to be seen, pushing their white bells through snow or chilly soil as early as the new year. Look out for varieties with larger flowers, frills or interesting green markings.
Hibbertia scandens (T)	Scrambler	Large bright yellow flowers and dark green leaves.
Hibiscus moscheutos (T)	1 m (3 ft)	Stunning blooms in a wide range of colours on slender stems.
Hyacinth	30–38 cm (12–15 in)	The 'Multiflora' varieties are best for tubs and containers and they produce several spikes of white, blue or pink: 'Pink Pearl' and 'Anna Marie' are pink; 'Carnegie' is white; 'City of Harlem' is yellow; the early 'Ostara' and 'Delft Blue' have blue spikes.
Muscari (Grape hyacinth)	15–20 cm (6–8 in)	The tiny grape hyacinth with its miniature spikes of deep, dark blue and delicate scent can look superb beneath other taller plants or fronting a window box display.

Narcissus	30–60 cm (12–24 in)	A wide range of colours and styles including double flowers, frills and special markings if you want to create a display of particular interest: N. 'Salome' has a pink crown; N. 'Marie Jose' is a butterfly type with yellow star-shaped markings; N. 'Petit-Four' is a double-flowered type with peach-coloured frilly centres.
N. asturiensis	7.5–10 cm (3–4 in)	Miniature early-flowering form with a wide range of flower types including tiny trumpet daffodils.
N. jonquilla	15–25 cm (6–10 in)	Sweet-scented variety that does well in tubs.
N. triandrus (Angel's tears)	15–40 cm (6–16 in)	A shorter growing, multi-headed variety with interesting flower shapes.
Primula	18 cm (7 in)	Popular for their dense display of bright flowers amongst thick green leaves. Many colour variations. The semi-miniature, early flowering primroses are prettiest for pots.
Scilla (Woodland bluebells)	10 cm (4 in)	Delicate nodding bells of blue, white and pink.
Tulipa	30–66 cm (12–26 in)	Valuable for adding exactly the colour you want later in the season since tulips are available in an extraordinary range of shades and shapes. There are single and double early blooms, special hybrids and late blooming types, exotic Parrot tulips, elegant lily-flowered varieties, blacks, reds, whites, blues, yellows – even stripes and frills.
T. greigii	15–30 cm (6–12 in)	A dwarf type good for window boxes and tubs and available in a range of colours: 'Princess Charmante' is scented, 'Red Riding Hood' is red with stripes.

An old barrel planted with a collection of primulas and sweet hyacinths makes a fragrant and colourful spring display.

PLANTS FOR SUMMER INTEREST

Alyssum	7.5–10 cm (3–4 in)	Makes a close-growing carpet of white or gold, useful for edging or softening the rim of containers. The white is handy for positioning with stronger deeper colours that need lightening.
Antirrhinum	20–30 cm (7.5–12 in)	Easy to grow in a wide range of colours – dwarf forms like 'Little Gem' are best for pots.
Begonia semperflorens	23–50 cm (9–18 in)	Valued for their combination of glossy green leaves and waxy flowers in shades of red, pink and white.
Calceolaria	25 cm (10 in)	Makes a mass of golden bubbles against green foliage.
Calendula officinalis (Pot marigold)	30–38 cm (12–15 in)	Reliable display of golden flowers and green foliage.
Campanula fragilis (Basket campanula)	Creeper	Trailing stems of large, pale blue flowers can look superb in pots and hanging baskets. Other forms have purple or dark blue flowers.
Chrysanthemum paludosum (Miniature marguerite)	23–30 cm (9–12 in)	Feathery green foliage studded with daisies.
Cineraria maritima	23–30 cm (9–12 in)	Prized for its crisp silver foliage, a good highlight and companion to other plants. Likes a sunny situation.
Coleus blumei	50 cm (20 in)	Strongly marked, coloured foliage plants in shades of dark red, yellow, green, cream and black.
Dianthus	25–120 cm (10–48 in)	Pretty pinks and carnations make a sweet-scented addition to old-fashioned tubs and pots in shades of pink, white and red.
Fuchsia	60 cm (24 in)	Many hybrid forms produce both large and small exotic dangling blooms in various combinations of purples, pinks and whites: excellent in hanging baskets and tubs.
Impatiens (Busy Lizzie)	25 cm (10 in)	Will tolerate cool shade to produce the familiar profusion of red, pink, white or striped flowers.
Limonium perezii (Statice) (T)	60 cm (24 in)	Large-leaved evergreen with masses of everlasting blue flowers.
Lobelia	30 cm (12 in)	The cascade types are perfect for hanging baskets, making a ball of pink or purple flowers.
Lysimachia nummularia (Creeping Jenny)	Creeper	Tiny green leaves and yellow flowers useful for window boxes and hanging baskets provided the soil is kept moist.
Mimulus (Monkey flower)	15–30 cm (6–12 in)	Good strong colour for window boxes and hanging baskets. The flowers are strong burgundy and gold, some of them interestingly blotched.

Pelargonium (Geranium)	30–38 cm (12–15 in)	Always popular plants for pots with their attractive foliage and red, pink and white flowers. Choose varieties specially recommended for growing in pots and tubs. The ivy-leaved types are good for hanging baskets; cascading and trailing types are useful for balconies and hanging baskets over which they can trail 46 cm (18 in).
Petunia	30 cm (12 in)	These compact forms are good for hanging baskets and produce a mass of frilled and sometimes striped trumpets of purple, pink, blue, red or yellow.
Salvia	25–30 cm (10–12 in)	Long-lasting and popular for the bright red spikes above marked green fleshy foliage.
Sedum sieboldii 'Variegatum'	Creeper	Pretty cream and blue or green foliage.
Tagetes	23 cm (9 in)	Many varieties forming mounds of tiny yellow, gold or bronze flowers among the dense, bright green feathery foliage.
Tagetes erecta (African marigold)	25–60 cm (10–24 in)	Large golden blooms are really eye-catching and plants come in a choice of sizes from tall standing at 60 cm (24 in), middling at 46–60 cm (18–24 in) and low-growing at 25–30 cm (10–12 in).
Tagetes patula (French marigold)	30 cm (12 in)	Splendid range of free-flowering golden blooms against feathery green foliage.
Tropaeolum majus (Nasturtium)	23 cm (9 in)	Attractive bright green leaves and gaily coloured yellow and orange flowers that flourish in poor soil and hot dry conditions. Height given here is for the shorter forms.
Verbena	15–30 cm (6–12 in)	Pointed leaves and flowers ranging from purple to scarlet or blue.
Viola (Pansy)	15–20 cm (6–8 in)	A great many different velvet colours and markings for creating special combinations.

ROSES

Large-flowered bush roses (Hybrid tea)	Low-growing types reach 75 cm (30 in)	Wide choice of colours: 'Abbeyfield' has a compact habit and is a soft red; small bushy 'Pot o' Gold' has scented yellow/gold flowers.
Cluster-flowered bush roses (Floribundas)	Smaller types to 45 cm (18 in)	Excellent colours and plenty of compact forms – includes patio roses: 'Elegant Pearl' is dense, compact and long flowering with creamy white flowers; 'Gentle Touch' produces pink flowers in clusters; 'Robin Redbreast' is dark red with a yellow or white eye.
Ramblers and climbers	1.8 m (6 ft)	Grow over a frame or trellis. 'Swany' has double white blooms and thrives in shade; 'Bobbie James' produces small, fragrant cream flowers; 'Paul's Scarlet Climber' is a semi-double brilliant red form.
Miniature roses	30 cm (12 in)	Pretty for small containers with delicate foliage and tiny pink, white or red flowers.

PLANTS FOR LATE SUMMER AND WINTER INTEREST

Begonia × *tuberhybrida* (Tuberous begonia)	30 cm (12 in)	Grand and colourful with their bright blooms: the pendula types are best for hanging baskets; choose 'Multiflora Maxima' for tubs.
Bergenia (Elephant's ears)	30 cm (12 in)	Mainly grown for the giant fleshy leaves but produces pretty white, pink or red flowers.
Chrysanthemum (Dwarf)	30–38 cm (12–15 in)	Pompom varieties in rich autumn shades of red and gold.
Colchicum autumnale	10–15 cm (4–6 in)	There are various free-flowering varieties producing mauve or white star-shaped flowers.
Crinum × *powellii*	60–90 cm (2–3 ft)	A tender plant for sheltered spots with amaryllis-like, huge scented trumpets of pink or white.
Cyclamen	7.5 cm (3 in)	There are various autumn- and winter-flowering types. The clusters of butterfly-like blooms in white or pink make an exotic splash of shape and colour. Some are scented.
Galtonia candicans	60–75 cm (24–30 in)	Produces spikes of white bell-like flowers.
Hardenbergia violacea (T)	Mat-forming	Makes a dense carpet of purple pea flowers from winter to spring.

When the ornamental can also become edible: tub-grown cos lettuce.

Iris danfordiae	5 cm (2 in)	Has yellow flowers.
Iris histrioides	5 cm (2 in)	Blue blooms in late autumn/winter.
Nerine bowdenii	45 cm (18 in)	Has lovely pink lily-like flowers.
Ranunculus	30 cm (12 in)	A wide variety of pinks, yellows and reds with a choice of double or semi-double forms.
Rhus succedanea (Wax tree) (T)	5 m (16 ft)	Brilliant red autumn foliage.
Scaevola aemula (T)	30 cm (12 in)	Good tub plant producing clusters of blue/purple flowers all year round.
Solanum capsicastrum (Winter cherry)	23–38 cm (9–15 in)	A good splash of colour for window boxes and small pots. The plants are like miniature green bushes studded with bright orange 'cherries'.
Sternbergia lutea	15 cm (6 in)	Has flowers similar to a yellow crocus.
Vallota speciosa (Scarborough lily)	60 cm (24 in)	A tender but spectacular plant for sheltered areas with its brilliant red trumpet flowers.
Zephyranthes candida	15–30 cm (6–12 in)	A tender plant with white starry flowers and grass-like leaves.

DWARF RHODODENDRONS AND AZALEAS

Japanese azaleas	50–75 cm (20–30 in)	Mostly evergreen or semi-evergreen but prone to damage from late frosts so protect from early morning sun. Range of colours includes 'Blue Danube' with striking blue blooms; 'Hinomayo' which makes a mass of pink flowers in late spring; or 'Johanna' which has bright red flowers against shiny dark green foliage.
Deciduous azaleas	1.2–1.5 m (4–5 ft)	Hardy with wonderful flowers and good autumn colour – allow them full sun or light shade. 'Persil' has white trumpets with an orange-yellow flare; 'Klondyke' has scented orange flowers and copper-coloured young foliage.
Dwarf rhododendrons	15–90 cm (6–35 in)	A wide choice of sizes, colours and forms. The compact and free-flowering *R. yakushimanum* hybrids include bright red against green, 'Dopey' and low-growing 'Grumpy' which has pink-tinged yellow trumpets. Also worth considering is tiny 'Chikor', a mass of yellow flowers in late spring at a height of 15–20 cm (6–8 in). Or unusual 'Ramapo' at 30–40 cm (12–16 in), which has glaucous green foliage and pale violet flowers.

Fruit can be grown on the roof garden as ornamental standard trees, dwarfed bushes or, in the case of strawberries, in special tiered pots or tubs.

EDIBLE PLANTS

Aubergine	90 cm (35 in)	'Slim Jim' is a decorative plant with purple leaves and small fruits 7 cm (3 in) long.
Corn salad	10 cm (4 in)	Sometimes called 'lambs' lettuce', this is a tasty salad plant that can be grown almost all year round. The narrow leaves are eaten young.
Mini cucumbers		Can grow indoors or on a sheltered patio in 25 cm (10 in) pots. 'Petita F' produces cucumbers 20 cm (8 in) long.
Dwarf French bean	30 cm (12 in)	'Royal Burgundy' has attractive purple flowers and purple pods so is decorative as well as useful.
Lettuce		Grow the more decorative varieties like 'Novita' which make an ornamental ball of curved leaves.
Olea europaea (T) (Olive)	5 m (16 ft)	Lime-preferring evergreen with Mediterranean-style grey-green foliage and edible fruits.
Peas	45 cm (18 in)	A dwarf, early variety like 'Hurst Beagle', which has a good flavour, could be grown in a container.
Sweet pepper	30–40 cm (12–16 in)	Plants with a dwarf habit like *Capsicum* 'Redskin F' are ideal for tubs and produce fruits around a central stem.
Radish	45 cm (18 in)	A tasty treat from the minimum of space: 'Cherry Bell' is a fast grower making round, red radishes. 'China Rose' is a winter radish, long and pink.
Tomatoes	45 cm (18 in)	Some varieties are perfect for pots or even strawberry containers. Choose a self-supporting type with fruits clustered round a central stem for growing in tubs, or one of the tiny cherry tomato types like the sweet-tasting 'Small Fry'.

The passion flower, Passiflora, is one of the most beautiful and exotic flowering climbers for balcony walls and trellis.

BALCONY CLIMBERS

Actinidia chinensis
(Chinese gooseberry)
Creamy-white flowers and large heart-shaped leaves. Likes plenty of sun and needs both male and female plants to produce the familiar hairy, egg-shaped edible fruits.

Aristolochia elegans (T)
(Dutchman's pipe)
Excellent climber for hanging below a pergola structure to show off the purple-blotched blooms and interesting seed pods.

Beaumontia grandiflora (T)
Grown for its beautifully scented long tubular white flowers.

Bougainvillea (T)
Classic Mediterranean and sub-tropical climber with masses of brilliantly coloured blooms.

Cissus discolor (T)
Fast-growing tropical twiner that needs some shade. Grown for its red foliage.

Clematis
A large number of types, both evergreen and deciduous, are grown for their spectacular range of flowers. Choose your own favourites from large or small blooms, scented, shade- or sun-lovers.

Clerodendrum thomsoniae
Climber producing masses of red and white flowers.

Clianthus puniceus (T)
(Lobster's claw)
Strangely shaped bright red flowers and evergreen foliage.

Holboellia coriacea
Dark green glossy evergreen with fragrant spring flowers and, sometimes, purple pod-like fruits.

Humulus lupulus (Hop)
A fast and useful climber; golden form 'Aureus' is particularly attractive.

Ipomoea rubrocaerulea
(Morning glory)
Grown for its short-lived but very pretty soft blue trumpet flowers from summer to autumn.

Jasminum nudiflorum
(Winter jasmine)
Delicate green foliage with flowers appearing on the naked branches during the winter.

Laburnum
Not strictly a climber, but the dripping golden blooms look superb hanging from a pergola or overhead trellis.

Lonicera (Honeysuckle)
There are various forms of this popular country climber, including evergreen and deciduous types, also night- or day-scented flowers.

Mandevilla × *amabilis* (T)
Night-flowering tropical twiner with pink tubular blooms.

Parthenocissus quinquefolia
(Virginia creeper)
Good foliage cover. The leaves turn a brilliant orange and scarlet in autumn.

Passiflora (Passion flower)
Large number of varieties, some of which are hardy others suited to sub-tropical conditions. Flowers are extraordinary. *P. edulis* bears edible fruit and is an excellent trellis smotherer.

Periploca graeca (Silk vine)	Fast-growing twiner with attractive deciduous dark green foliage.
Polygonum baldschuanicum (Russian vine)	Excellent fast grower for quick cover. Late-summer flowers make a mass of white frothy panicles.
Schisandra chinensis	Shade-preferring twiner with scented early summer flowers of pink or white.
Solanum crispum	Vigorous lime-lover with blue/purple flowers.
Thunbergia alata (Black-eyed Susan)	Rampant twiner with white or yellow flowers with dark purple centres.
Trachelospermum jasminoides	Evergreen climber with fragrant creamy-white blooms. *T. asiaticum* is hardier and more compact.
Tropaeolum speciosum (Nasturtium)	A bright-flowered annual producing a mass of red and gold flowers among large green leaves.
Vitis vinifera (Grape vine)	A useful foliage climber. 'Purpurea' has claret to deep purple foliage.
Wattakaka sinensis	Twining shrub grown for its scented white flowers with red dots. Evergreen in milder climates, frost-hardy down to $-5°C$ (22°F).
Wisteria sinensis	Long racemes of scented lilac flowers and delicate foliage look superb on wall, trellis or pergola.

IVIES

Hedera canariensis (Canary Island ivy)	Large leaves which turn bronze in winter. Silvery grey and cream-white variegated forms also available.
H. colchica 'Dentata' (Persian ivy)	Particularly large leaves: variety 'Sulphur Heart' has yellow splashes, 'Variegata' has creamy yellow margins.
H. helix (Common English ivy)	Useful ivy that will grow almost anywhere, even in very shady conditions. There are many variations:
H. h. 'Cavendishii'	Small mottled grey leaves with cream margins.
H. h. 'Chicago'	Small leaves blotched with bronze-purple.
H. h. 'Deltoidea'	Heart-shaped leaves making dense cover that turns bronze in winter.
H. h. 'Glacier'	Silver grey with white margins.
H. h. 'Goldheart'	Central yellow splash to each leaf.
H. h. 'Manda's Crested'	Slow grower with reddish colour in winter.
H. h. 'Marginata Elegantissima'	Small grey-green leaves that have pink edges in winter.
H. h. 'Sagittifolia'	Interestingly shaped five-lobed leaves. There is a cream variegated form.

A small but prolific kitchen roof garden featuring fruits, vegetables and herbs in window boxes, hanging baskets, grow-bags and other containers. The inclusion of a few traditional flowering plants such as marigolds, sweet-scented pinks and tobacco plants not only encourages bees and butterflies, but creates more of a cottage garden atmosphere.

HERBS

Bush basil	25 cm (10 in)	*Ocimum minimum* is best for pots with small compact foliage.
Chives	23 cm (9 in)	Their spiky grass-like foliage and pink pompom flowers are a good contrast to other plants.
Garlic chives	30 cm (12 in)	Chives with a mild garlic onion flavour and white flowers.
Marjoram	25–30 cm (10–12 in)	An attractive bush of small leaves and soft pink flowers.
Mint	15 cm (6 in)	Many varieties with different scents and flavours and including variegated foliage types. Container growing helps to limit vigorous growth which normally makes mints unsuitable in the garden.
Parsley	15–30 cm (6–12 in)	'Curlina' is a tightly curled compact form, dark green and very attractive – ideal for pots.
Rosemary	60–120 cm (24–48 in)	An excellent shrubby bush of spiky foliage and soft blue flowers.
Sage	30 cm (12 in)	Soft grey or purple foliage plant although it does produce attractive flowers in summer.
Savory	30–45 cm (12–18 in)	Summer and winter varieties make an attractive small-leaved plant. A useful pot herb.
Tarragon	1 m (3 ft)	The French type has the better flavour. Narrow flat green leaves make an attractive plant.
Thyme	23–30 cm (9–12 in)	Many varieties offer variegated and coloured foliage forms, including creeping thymes which are excellent plants for softening the edges of pots.

INDEX

Readers should also refer to the Plant Lists (pp. 116–41) for individual plant information.

ACKNOWLEDGEMENTS

The Publishers are grateful to the following agencies for granting permission to reproduce the colour photographs: The Garden Picture Library (pages 7, 10, 15, 19, 22, 23, 26, 27, 39, 42, 43, 46, 51, 55, 58/59, 63, 74, 82, 87, 90, 95, 99, 102/3, 107, 110, 119, 122, 131, 135, 138) and Elizabeth Whiting Associates (pages 11, 14/15, 30, 34, 66, 79, 94), Clive Nichols (designer Randle Siddeley) 71.

All the line drawings were drawn by Mike Shoebridge.